PHYSICIANS
IN
BUREAUCRACY

This is a volume in the Arno Press collection

DISSERTATIONS ON SOCIOLOGY

Advisory Editors
Harriet Zuckerman
Robert K. Merton

See last pages of this volume for a complete list of titles

PHYSICIANS
IN
BUREAUCRACY

A Case Study of Professional Pressures
on Organizational Roles

Mary E. Weber Goss

ARNO PRESS
A New York Times Company
New York • 1980

Publisher's Note: This book has been reproduced from the best available copy.

Editorial Supervision: Doris Krone

———

First Publication 1980 by Arno Press Inc.
Copyright © 1959 by Mary E. Weber Goss
Printed by permission of Mary E. Weber Goss
DISSERTATIONS ON SOCIOLOGY
ISBN for complete set: 0-405-12945-9
See last pages of this volume for titles.
Manufactured in the United States of America

———

Library of Congress Cataloging in Publication Data

Goss, Mary E   Weber, 1926-
  Physicians in bureaucracy.

  (Dissertations in sociology)
  Originally presented as the author's thesis,
Columbia University, 1959.
  Bibliography: p.
  1.   Medical centers--Sociological aspects.
2.   Physicians. 3.   Bureaucracy. 4.   Social role.
I.   Title.   II.   Series.
RA965.G67   1980   610.69'6   79-9002
ISBN 0-405-12971-8

PHYSICIANS IN BUREAUCRACY:

A CASE STUDY OF PROFESSIONAL PRESSURES ON ORGANIZATIONAL ROLES

by

Mary E. Weber Goss

Submitted in partial fulfillment.
of the requirements for the degree
of Doctor of Philosophy, in the
Faculty of Political Science,
Columbia University

1959

ACKNOWLEDGMENTS

Professor Robert K. Merton provided invaluable advice and constructive criticism in all phases of this study, from its beginning some six years ago to the present. Helpful counsel concerning procedures for collection and analysis of the materials was given by Dr. Patricia L. Kendall, and Professor Hans L. Zetterberg offered fruitful suggestions about the analysis of authority and influence relationships. Professor Charles R. Wright, formerly at Columbia University and now at the University of California in Los Angeles, contributed incisive comments on virtually every aspect of the project. David Caplovitz, Research Fellow at the Bureau of Applied Social Research of Columbia University, generously made available important unpublished data from his own investigation of physicians. These several debts are acknowledged with pleasure and gratitude.

With equal gratitude the author is pleased to acknowledge the help of physicians and other staff members at The New York Hospital – Cornell Medical Center. Although each cannot be named individually, a considerable number contributed directly or indirectly to this study: some by volunteering information and answering questions, others by allowing observation of their work. Dr. George G. Reader, Director of the Comprehensive Care and Teaching Program in the Center, served simultaneously as esteemed colleague and valuable critic. Together with his associates in the Program, he also provided many useful insights into the nature of the medical subculture. Dr. David P. Barr, Professor of Medicine and Chairman of the Advisory Committee of the Comprehensive Care and Teaching Program when the study began, gave initial permission for participant observation in the Program and offered encouragement beyond the call of his office. These men and their colleagues are not responsible, of course, for any inadvertent errors in fact or interpretation that this report may contain.

Finally, through financial aid given to the Comprehensive Care and Teaching Program as well as to the Bureau of Applied Social Research of Columbia University, The Commonwealth Fund indirectly supported a large part of this study. Appreciation for such support is warmly extended.

TABLE OF CONTENTS

LIST OF TABLES

LIST OF FIGURES

ABSTRACT

PHYSICIANS IN BUREAUCRACY:
A CASE STUDY OF PROFESSIONAL PRESSURES
ON ORGANIZATIONAL ROLES

Mary E. Weber Goss

Sociologists have held that bureaucratic and professional norms tend to be incompatible if not contradictory. It
has therefore been assumed that professionals at work in bureaucratic organizations experience strain and tension in living up
to their diverse obligations. Yet little empirical evidence
has been assembled to test this assumption. Moreover, it is
possible that professionals affect as well as are affected by
bureaucratic forms of organization. The present investigation
explores this possibility in the case of a group of physicians
forming a division of a hospital. The study takes as problem-
atic the occurrence of strains resulting from contradictions
between the requirements of organizational and professional
roles, and tries to search out structural mechanisms that serve
to reconcile such contradictions.

Data were gathered primarily through intermittent participant observation over a period of five years (1952-1957),
and secondarily through study of organizational documents and
questionnaires filled out by physicians. The research site is

the Comprehensive Care and Teaching Program (CC&TP) of the New York Hospital - Cornell Medical Center. Located mainly in two out-patient clinics, the CC&TP yearly provides medical care for several thousand patients and clinical instruction for all fourth-year medical students at Cornell. Along with a small number of nurses, social workers, and other hospital personnel, some eighty physicians participate in the Program. Most of these physicians serve on a part-time unpaid basis but some are salaried full-time employees; all are on the staffs of both the Hospital and the Medical College.

The investigation centered on two areas of potential strain and adjustment: authority and the division of labor. In both areas, bureaucratic and professional norms and practices proved to be closely interwoven in ways that apparently produced relatively few tensions and little strain for the physicians in the organization.

Physicians were hierarchically organized in order to facilitate coordination and supervision of their work. The hierarchy was basically regulated by professional standards. In the sphere of administration, physicians in formally superordinate positions could and did exercise authoritative control; as is generally true of bureaucracies, formal rank was the basis for effective authority in strictly administrative matters. But when physicians of higher rank in the bureaucracy supervised the care given patients by other physicians, they took the role of consultant and offered only advice rather than

imposing orders. Such advice could be legitimately accepted or
rejected, depending on the physician's own professional judgment. In this sphere, the technical expertness of a physician
was the primary basis for his right to offer advice. As is
generally true of bureaucracy also, work was divided among physicians in the CC&TP according to their specialized qualifications. Yet in accord with professional values concerning the
importance of self-government as well as of giving service,
physicians rather than specially-trained lay administrators
held the major administrative posts and regularly combined
these duties with more professional activities (service, teaching, research).

These and related findings provide the basis for the
following conclusions, which are put forward as hypotheses for
systematic investigation in formal organizations composed primarily of physicians or other professionals. (1) Professional
norms and values set distinct limits to the ways in which
organizational needs for policy-making, coordination, and
supervision are met, and thus markedly affect the definition of
organizational roles. (2) To reconcile professional norms and
values with organizational needs, certain non-bureaucratic
structural mechanisms are required. These include (a) a system
of dual control (formal authority and formal advisory relations)
within a single hierarchy of positions, where those with higher
formal rank (b) have sufficient technical competence to qualify
as expert consultants in the eyes of the professionals whose

work they supervise, and (c) are assigned professional as well
as administrative duties so that the latter occupy only part of
their working time. (3) An organization with these characteristics can be classified as a semi-bureaucracy; it is a combination of the pattern Gouldner has described as "representative"
bureaucracy and the pattern identified in this study as
"advisory" bureaucracy.

CHAPTER I

INTRODUCTION

This is an exploratory analysis of some aspects of the work relationships among an organized group of physicians in a large medical center. More broadly, it is a study of organizational roles as they are conditioned by professional norms, values, and work requirements. The empirical content of the analysis is based primarily on intermittent participant observation over a period of five years; the analysis itself is based on sociological theory concerning bureaucracy and the professions.

Points of Departure

The type of organization that Max Weber[1] described as bureaucracy has long appeared to be at odds with the work requirements, norms, and values of professionals. In brief, bureaucracy is a rational, efficient organization of statuses, characterized by hierarchical authority, division of labor on the basis of specialized competence, systematic rules, and

---

[1] H. H. Gerth and C. Wright Mills (tr.), From Max Weber: Essays in Sociology (New York: Oxford University Press, 1946), pp. 196-264; A. M. Henderson and Talcott Parsons (tr.), Max Weber: The Theory of Social and Economic Organization (New York: Oxford University Press, 1947), pp. 324-423.

impersonality.[1] The professional, however, is a recognized master of a particular body of knowledge and practice as a result of prolonged and specialized intellectual training, and he is committed to using his knowledge and skills in accordance with standards set by the profession to which he belongs.[2]

Far from condoning the hierarchical authority roles characteristic of bureaucracy, his work norms emphasize self-government for the profession as a whole and autonomy for each practitioner within the limits laid down by the profession. Further, hard-and-fast bureaucratic rules that apply to all alike do not allow for dealing with the exceptional case, and it is precisely the exceptional case that professionals more than any other occupational group are most likely to encounter in the course of their work. While the professional is enjoined to treat all alike according to need and in this sense to be impersonal and to abide by general rules, his impersonality must always be conditioned by his judgment as to the needs of the particular case under consideration and the "rules" he must take into account are those of the profession rather than of any particular bureaucracy. Only in the realm of specialization and the division of labor does there seem to

[1] This is Blau's capsule summary of the more detailed formulations advanced by Weber which are cited in the preceding note. See Peter M. Blau, Bureaucracy in Modern Society (New York: Random House, 1956), p. 19.

[2] A. M. Carr-Saunders and P. A. Wilson, The Professions (Oxford: Clarendon Press, 1933), pp. 284-313; see also "Professions," Encyclopedia of the Social Sciences, Vol. 12, pp. 476-80.

be agreement between bureaucratic standards and professional
norms; as specialists themselves, professionals are committed
to the division of labor according to specialized competence.
However, they are also committed to self-government — as has
been indicated — and therefore they are likely to set aside
the requirement of trained, specialized competence in the case
of administrative activity.

Taking note of such contradictions as well as of the
growing number of professionals who work in apparently bureaucratic contexts, students of the professions have repeatedly
stressed the need for empirical research to determine the kinds
of adjustments or alternative tensions that occur when the two
are confronted.[1]

In considering the kinds of adjustments or tensions that
may ensue, what has been learned in other contexts has been
less often stressed. Recent research in the sociology of complex organization[2] indicates that actual patterns of

---

[1]Talcott Parsons, "Introduction," in A. M. Henderson
and T. Parsons, op. cit., pp. 58-60; Robert K. Merton, Social
Theory and Social Structure (revised and enlarged ed.; Glencoe,
Ill.: The Free Press, 1957), pp. 123-27 and pp. 207-24; Logan
Wilson, The Academic Man (New York: Oxford University Press,
1942), pp. 71-93; Bernard Barber, Science and the Social Order
(Glencoe, Ill.: The Free Press, 1952), pp. 144-46 and pp. 167-
69; Mary Jean Huntington, "Sociology of Professions, 1945-55,"
in Hans L. Zetterberg (ed.), Sociology in the United States of
America (Paris: UNESCO, 1956), pp. 87-93; William J. Goode,
Robert K. Merton, and Mary Jean Huntington, The Professions in
American Society: A Sociological Analysis and Casebook (forth-
coming).

[2]Philip Selznick, TVA and the Grass Roots (Berkeley:
University of California Press, 1953); Alvin W. Gouldner,

bureaucratic structure and operation are less rigid and more
variable than the ideal type Weber outlined, and that his conception of bureaucracy needs to be extended accordingly. Likewise, research in the sociology of the professions[1] suggests
that there are wider ranges of permissible behavior open to
professional persons than might be assumed from their ethical
codes or public statements. Together, the two sets of observations imply that there may be somewhat more room for mutual adjustment of professional norms and bureaucratic standards than
has generally been supposed.

Studies which specifically investigate this possibility
are rare. No doubt partly because of the nature of the particular cases examined, available analyses and studies have
tended to focus either on the professional or on the organizational structure as the major site for adjustments or tensions.

Patterns of Industrial Bureaucracy (Glencoe: The Free Press,
1954); Peter M. Blau, The Dynamics of Bureaucracy (Chicago: The
University of Chicago Press, 1955); Roy G. Francis and Robert
C. Stone, Service and Procedure in Bureaucracy (Minneapolis:
The University of Minnesota Press, 1956).

[1]Gene N. Levine, Natalie Rogoff, and David Caplovitz,
"Diversities in Role Conceptions," (Bureau of Applied Social
Research, Columbia University, 1955, dittoed); Gene N. Levine,
"The Good Physician," (Bureau of Applied Social Research,
Columbia University, 1957, mimeographed); Harold L. Wilensky,
Intellectuals in Labor Unions (Glencoe, Ill.: The Free Press,
1956), pp. 129-44; Renée C. Fox, "Physicians and Patients on a
Research Ward: A Study of Stress and Ways of Coming to Terms
with Stress," (unpublished Ph.D. dissertation, Radcliffe
College, Harvard University, 1953); Robert K. Merton, "Some
Preliminaries to a Sociology of Medical Education," in Robert
K. Merton, George G. Reader, and Patricia L. Kendall (eds.),
The Student-Physician (Cambridge: Harvard University Press,
1957), pp. 3-79, at pp. 71-79.

Thus Merton,[1] Field,[2] Wilensky,[3] and Ben-David[4] have paid primary attention to the impact of bureaucratic requirements on professional norms, values, and behavior. Parsons,[5] Wilson,[6] and others,[7] however, have reversed this focus and attended more to the problem of how the professional's demands may affect the overall network of roles that constitutes bureaucratic organization. Neither approach logically excludes the other, of course. They are obviously complementary, and the present study assumes that both are required for adequate understanding of the case in hand.

With specific reference to the professional group this study concerns -- physicians -- several recent sociological investigations of American hospitals[8] explicitly or implicitly

---

[1] Robert K. Merton, "Role of the Intellectual in Public Bureaucracy," op. cit. (1957), pp. 207-24.

[2] Mark G. Field, Doctor and Patient in Soviet Russia (Cambridge: Harvard University Press, 1957).

[3] Harold L. Wilensky, op. cit.

[4] Joseph Ben-David, "The Professional Role of the Physician in Bureaucratized Medicine: A Study in Role Conflict," (mimeographed, 1957).

[5] Talcott Parsons, "Suggestions for a Sociological Approach to the Theory of Organizations- II," Administrative Science Quarterly, Vol. 1, No. 2 (Sept., 1956), pp. 225-39, esp. pp. 235-37.

[6] Logan Wilson, op. cit.

[7] See the hospital studies cited in following footnote.

[8] A. H. Stanton and M. H. Schwartz, The Mental Hospital (New York: Basic Books Inc., 1954); Harvey L. Smith, "The Sociological Study of Hospitals" (unpublished Ph.D.

suggest that in such a setting physicians affect the organizational structure more than they are affected by it. These investigations indicate that while physicians are not generally employed by the hospital, they are functionally necessary for the hospital's continued operation; though they are ordinarily productive workers rather than administrators, by virtue of their profession they enjoy higher prestige than those in other occupations who may officially operate the hospital; and even though physicians hold staff positions which are nominally outside the line organization of authority in the hospital, their qualifications as medical experts enable them to exert influence and authority with regard to the behavior of all levels of hospital personnel. They are, in other words, in a strategic position to enforce their professional demands, and it would seem that the burden of adjustment -- or its alternative, unresolved tension -- consequently falls heavily on their co-workers in the hospital: nurses, technicians, administrators, trustees, and other personnel. As Harvey Smith[1] has remarked, the formally bureaucratic structure of hospitals actually

---

dissertation, University of Chicago, 1949); Albert F. Wessen, "The Social Structure of a Modern Hospital," (unpublished Ph.D. dissertation, Yale University, 1951); Temple Burling, Edith M. Lentz, and Robert N. Wilson, The Give and Take in Hospitals (New York: G. P. Putnam's Sons, 1956); Edith M. Lentz, "The American Voluntary Hospital as an Example of Institutional Change," (unpublished Ph.D. dissertation, Cornell University, 1956); Paul Barrabee, "A Study of a Mental Hospital," (unpublished Ph.D. dissertation, Harvard University, 1951).

[1]Harvey L. Smith, "Two Lines of Authority are One Too Many," Modern Hospital, Vol. 84, No. 3 (March, 1955), pp. 59-64.

involves "built-in conflicts," with physicians and their professional norms more often than not emerging the victors.[1]

These findings turn attention to the structure of the
hospital's professional medical staff itself as a fruitful area
for inquiry, and to organizational arrangements in which physicians are formally responsible for supervision and coordination
of the work of other physicians. There are few empirical
sociological studies of this kind of situation,[2] yet there is
reason to believe they would provide valuable information for
students of the professions and of complex organization alike.
For in such instances the factor of professional medical training, together with the prestige and authority it entails relative to other occupations, is automatically held constant, with
the result that differences in this regard cannot be utilized
to explain or account for the nature of the structure (as they
have been in the case of the hospital as a whole). The mutual
impact of professional norms and organizational requirements
can therefore be examined in fairly "pure" form; adjustments or
tensions which are inherent in the supervision and coordination

---

[1] For a case in which the reverse seems to be true, see
Mark G. Field, op. cit. For some impressionistic evidence that
physicians in American hospitals are becoming more subject to
bureaucratic controls than previously, see Edith Lentz, op. cit.

[2] See, however, Oswald Hall, "Stages of a Medical
Career," American Journal of Sociology, Vol. LIII, No. 5 (March,
1948), pp. 327-37, and "The Informal Organization of the Medi-
cal Profession," Canadian Journal of Economics and Political
Science, Vol. XII, No. 1 (Feb., 1946), pp. 30-44; also Rose
Laub Coser, "Authority and Decision-Making in a Hospital,"
American Sociological Review, Vol. 23, No. 1 (Feb., 1958), pp.
56-63.

of professional work can be singled out from those which are merely artifacts of laypersons' attempts to control the activities of experts.

Precisely because a professional medical staff is occupationally homogeneous, of course, it might be expected that their organizational role relationships would exhibit more adjustments than tensions. But as this study will suggest, it would be a mistake to assume that no adjustments need occur, or that the norms which govern physicians' intra-professional relationships in private practice will find their exact counterpart in an organizational setting. As Wilson has indicated with respect to the organization of teachers in American universities, the sheer facts of size and the need for coordination of many complex activities make complete individualism and autonomy on the part of each professional impossible.[1]

Research Problems

Guided by the considerations that have been detailed, this study takes the apparent incompatibility between bureaucratic standards and professional norms as a point of departure for exploring certain of the actual norms, values, and behavior of a group of physicians who were members of an organized professional staff. In this exploration, the existence of strains resulting from contradictions between organizational role requirements and professional role requirements is considered

---

[1]Logan Wilson, op. cit., pp. 72-92.

problematical, as is the existence of structural mechanisms
which serve in some measure to reconcile differences where they
exist. Examination of data bearing on these problems in turn
indirectly sheds some light on the larger problem of how the
professional affects and is affected by bureaucracy.

Out of the several that might have been selected, two
areas of potential strain and adjustment are described and
analyzed in this study: hierarchical authority and the specialized division of labor. These areas were initially chosen for
investigation because they appeared to represent extremes that
could be usefully contrasted; professional norms seemed most in
accord with the latter characteristic of bureaucracy, and least
in accord with the former characteristic. However, as will be
seen, this view greatly over-simplified the situation with
respect to the division of labor.

The Research Setting

The New York Hospital - Cornell Medical Center, where
this study took place, is composed of Cornell University Medical College, The New York Hospital, and the Cornell University-
New York Hospital School of Nursing. Along with other personnel,
nearly 700 physicians are associated with the former two
institutions. About 80 of these physicians participated in a
special program of out-patient care and teaching, the Comprehensive Care and Teaching Program (CC&TP). This Program constituted a sub-organization in the Medical Center and the major
base of fieldwork for the present study.

The nature of the Program is described in detail in the
following chapter. Here it may be noted that each year several
thousand patients received medical care under the auspices of
the Program, and from 30 to 35 fourth-year medical students
received clinical instruction. In contrast with in-patient
care and teaching which requires the services of numerous
ancillary workers, like most out-patient services the Program
involved only a small number of nurses, social workers, and
other hospital personnel.

Thus apart from the ever-changing aggregate of patients
and students, physicians themselves constituted the most numerous group in the Program, and their work-associates consisted
to a great extent of fellow-physicians. Moreover, in the
Program as in the Hospital and the Medical college of which it
was a part, the physicians composed an organized staff, with
differential rights, duties, and privileges attached to their
respective positions, whether full-time or part-time, high or
low rank, salaried or unsalaried. As later chapters will show
in detail, physicians not only participated in the program in
the traditional "staff" sense; some were "line" officials as
well, with official responsibility for supervising, coordinating, and planning the activities of others in the Program.

The Program was not long-established or immutably fixed
when the observer first came on the scene in 1952. It was, in
fact, just beginning, and noticeable changes in organization
which involved physicians took place over the ensuing five

years.

In part, then, the fieldwork situation itself directed
attention to the structure of relationships among physicians as
a significant area for investigation. And the length of time
during which the course of the Program was followed permitted
examination of the interplay between physicians' professional
norms and values, on the one hand, and their organizational
roles and behavior on the other, in a way that would not otherwise have been possible.

From the outset it should be recognized that the case
to be reported is probably atypical in a number of respects.
There is scattered evidence to suggest that out of the approximately 205,000 physicians in the United States in 1950, not all
were affiliated with hospitals,[1] less than half were certified
medical specialists (rather than general practitioners),[2] and
considerably fewer held teaching appointments in a medical
school.[3] The group of physicians whom this study concerns,
however, were all specialists with teaching appointments as
well as hospital affiliations. Moreover, in 1956 only about

---

[1]Hospital Council of Greater New York, Hospital Staff
Appointments of Physicians in New York City (New York: The
Macmillan Co., 1951), pp. 12-19.

[2]Frank G. Dickinson, Distribution of Medical School
Alumni in the United States as of April, 1950, Bulletin 101,
Bureau of Medical Economic Research, A.M.A. (Chicago: American
Medical Association, 1956), p. 11.

[3]John E. Deitrick and Robert C. Berson, Medical Schools
in the United States at Mid-Century (New York: McGraw-Hill Book
Co., Inc., 1953), p. 195.

one-tenth of the nearly 7,000 hospitals listed by the American Hospital Association[1] were approved for training both interns and residents[2] -- as was The New York Hospital -- and almost none was closely involved with a medical school in conducting a program for out-patient care and teaching similar to that reported in this study.[3]

The major purpose of a case study is not to provide generalizations, however, but to explore new areas of scientific inquiry and to suggest hypotheses for future systematic investigation. Since there can be little doubt that the trend in medical practice -- as well as in professional practice generally -- is toward more rather than less organization and specialization,[4] there will clearly be increasing opportunities to investigate the hypotheses which emerge from analysis of the particular case in hand.

---

[1] "Hospital Statistics," Hospitals, J.A.H.A., Vol. 32, No. 15 (August 1, 1958), p. 364.

[2] Journal of the American Medical Association, Vol. 165, No. 5 (Oct. 5, 1957), p. 460.

[3] The closest parallel to the CC&TP was undertaken at the University of Colorado School of Medicine; see Fred Kern, Jr., "The General Medical Clinic of the University of Colorado. An Experiment in Medical Education and Medical Care," American Journal of Public Health, Vol. 45, No. 1 (Jan. 1955), pp. 47-52.

[4] C. Wright Mills, White Collar (New York: Oxford University Press, 1951); Roy Lewis and Angus Maude, Professional People in England (Cambridge: Harvard University Press, 1953); H. G. Weiskotten and Marion E. Altenderfer, "Trends in Medical Practice," Journal of Medical Education, Vol. 31, No. 7 (July, 1956), Part 2.

Methods of Investigation

Empirical materials for this study were collected
mainly through participant observation, but questionnaires and
official documents were also used.

Entree to the research setting was provided by the
Director of the Program, a physician who was interested in obtaining objective information which would ultimately aid in
evaluating the accomplishments of the organization.[1] His
initial and continuing sponsorship was vital in obtaining
access to situations in the Medical College and in the Hospital
that are ordinarily closed to persons without medical training.

Over the span of five years the writer served as participant observer in the Program for varying periods of time.
The first period covered fourteen months, from June 1952 to
July 1953. It was followed by an observation period of one
week in July 1954, another week in February 1956, and a final
six-month period which began in February 1957 and ended in July
of that year.

Within the two longer periods, the observer spent an

<hr>

[1]The first phase of this study was part of a larger
research program in the sociology of medical education, conducted by the Bureau of Applied Social Research, Columbia University, in collaboration with Cornell University Medical
College. For description of how this collaboration came about,
see George G. Reader, "The Cornell Comprehensive Care and
Teaching Program," in R. K. Merton, G. G. Reader, and P. L.
Kendall, op. cit., pp. 81-101, at pp. 90-92. In the same
volume, Merton analyzes the broad trends in medical education
and in sociology leading to such programs of research; see "Some
Preliminaries to a Sociology of Medical Education," pp. 3-79.

average of three days each week in the medical setting. During
the first period her role in the program was almost exclusively
that of a passive observer; she "participated" in the various
medical conferences, staff meetings, lectures, and seminars
only in the sense of being present. In informal situations,
such as conversations over coffee or lunch or in the hall of
the clinic, she often interviewed staff members about themselves and their work, but as a matter of policy offered no
advice or evaluative comments concerning their activities or
any aspect of the program. After an initial short period of
wariness and reticence on the part of staff members, interaction between members of this group and the observer was
generally friendly and relaxed. Four years later, during the
final six-month period, relationships with staff members were
similarly congenial, but the observer's role had changed from
passive to active participation in the program. Formally
designated Consultant in Sociology to the program, she had
duties which included giving occasional advice to staff members, although not, of course, concerning the care of patients.

Participant observation is not yet well codified as a
research technique, nor is there currently complete agreement
among sociologists concerning the circumstances that incontro-
vertibly call for its use.[1] That the method is particularly

[1] For some recent differences of opinion in this regard,
see Howard Becker and Blanche Geer, "Participant Observation
and Interviewing: a Comparison," Human Organization, Vol. 16,
No. 3 (Fall, 1957), pp. 28-32, and the "Comment" on this

suited for exploration of complex social situations nevertheless seems clear, as does the advantage it holds over other
methods with respect to providing immediate, first-hand information about events that subjects might not remember, or consider too commonplace or private to report in a formal inter-
view with an outsider. For both of these reasons participant
observation was desirable in the present study. The method
proved essential as a means of orienting the observer to the
nature and nuances of the medical subculture, and helped
markedly in the process of realistically defining the problems
under investigation. The observer was initially almost totally
ignorant of how an out-patient teaching clinic functions, and
of physicians' work routines and responsibilities in such a
setting. It was of course necessary to learn such basic facts
before substantive points of potential stress between professional norms and organizational requirements could be examined
intensively. Early interviews with those in charge proved inadequate in this regard, not so much because physicians viewed
the information as private or confidential as because their
verbal descriptions took for granted a wealth of background
knowledge which the observer did not have. To be told, for
example, that a major duty of physicians in the clinic was to

article by Martin Trow in the same volume, pp. 33-35. For a
general description of participant observation as a research
technique, see Marie Jahoda, Morton Deutsch, and Stuart W.
Cook, Research Methods in Social Relations (New York: The
Dryden Press, 1951), Part I, pp. 134-44.

"check students' work-ups of patients" was not very informative
until the behavior involved had been both further explained and
independently observed, since the explanation by itself was
likely to involve further terms which had meaning for the physicians but not for the observer. For instance, each of the
underlined terms in the following explanations offered by a
physician has a very specific meaning in the medical subculture,
a meaning which could only be partly grasped by further "explanations": "A work-up is taking a history and doing a physical";
"In checking a student you ask him to present the case, and you
explore with him the diagnostic or management problems that
seem to be involved; then you personally check his physical
findings, and help him formulate the problem." Continuing observation, therefore, had to be interwoven with repeated informal interviewing of staff members to gain a working famili-
arity with everyday events. Once the particular foci of the
investigation were determined, participant observation of this
sort remained a useful procedure for collecting more specific
information, as for example, in ascertaining differences
between patterns of professional supervision on the wards and
in the clinic.

However, participant observation cannot provide data
concerning the prevalence of a particular norm or value among a
large number of people. For such information, this study
occasionally draws on the unpublished findings of a questionnaire survey of physicians, conducted in 1956 by David Caplovitz

of the Bureau of Applied Social Research, Columbia University.[1]
Mailed to all 604 physicians on the faculty of Cornell Medical
College who were actively engaged in at least some teaching at
the time of the survey, the questionnaire was filled out by 507
respondents, a return of 84 per cent.

The official records of the Program were also consulted
for information bearing on organizational roles and events.
Most useful in this regard were the mimeographed Annual Reports,
which contain accounts written by core staff members concerning
yearly accomplishments, deficiencies, changes and additions in
personnel, as well as statements of specific organizational
objectives. Finally, publications describing various aspects
of the Program proved helpful, especially in outlining the
formal structure of the organization. These publications are
cited where relevant.

---

[1]A copy of the questionnaire is reproduced in the
Appendix. As is noted there, the survey represents part of the
continuing study of medical education undertaken by the Bureau
of Applied Social Research. For a brief preliminary description of Caplovitz's study design -- which involves comparison
of faculty attitudes, norms, and values with those of their
students -- see R. K. Merton, G. G. Reader, and P. L. Kendall,
op. cit., pp. 295-96.
The Bureau of Applied Social Research also conducted
two earlier surveys of the opinions of Cornell faculty physicians. In these surveys, interviews rather than questionnaires
were used; the first occurred in 1953 and, being exploratory,
involved only 32 physicians; see David Caplovitz, "Report on
Faculty Opinions," unpublished manuscript, 1953 (in the files
of the Bureau of Applied Social Research, Columbia University).
The second covered a sample of some 90 physicians and occurred
in 1954; see Gene N. Levine, Natalie Rogoff, and David
Caplovitz, op. cit. The background provided by both of these
reports was of course useful in the present study.

Overview of the Report

Five chapters follow. Chapter II describes how the
CC&TP came into being and it outlines the formal organization
of the Program at two points in time: when it began in 1952 and
again in 1957, after it had been in existence for five years.
Particular attention is paid to the official supervisory responsibilities that were attached to certain positions, and to
changes in the number and nature of such positions.

Chapter III uses case materials and survey data as the
basis for analyzing the role expectations which physicians had
concerning the ways in which supervisory responsibilities were
to be discharged. Two distinct types of supervisory control
relationships are seen to exist, each supported by specifiable
values which physicians hold and each institutionalized as
appropriate for a particular sphere of work.

Chapter IV continues the analysis of one of the types
of control, the formal advisory relationship. This is the type
that applies to professional work; in certain respects it is
found to run counter to its closest parallel in private
practice, the consultation relationship. Data are therefore
examined in order to determine some of the conditions under
which physicians will nevertheless find the advisory relationship acceptable.

Chapter V moves away from the problem of control relationships and views administration as a problem in the division
of labor. It reviews the conflicting values physicians held

concerning this activity and shows how these are related to the actual distribution of administrative work among physicians of varying statuses and ranks. Attention is also given to the matter of how physicians may become motivated to engage in administration; in this connection a tentative typology of administrative tasks is presented.

Finally, Chapter VI brings together the findings of the preceding chapters and analyzes their implications with respect to the larger problems with which the study began. The concept of "advisory bureaucracy" emerges from the analysis, as do certain directives for future research concerning professionals who work in organizational settings.

CHAPTER II

FORMAL ORGANIZATION AND THE PROFESSIONAL

In bureaucracy, as Max Weber notes, the staff is composed of trained experts and "the organization of offices
follows the principle of hierarchy; that is, each lower office
is under the control and supervision of a higher one."[1]
Whether the hierarchical principle can be applied feasibly to
the formal organization of experts who are professionals, however, is problematical. The nature of professional work is
such that professionals must make complex decisions for which
they are held personally responsible, not only by their professional colleagues and society at large, but by themselves as
well. Thus even though they work in an organizational setting
they require what Logan Wilson has called "individual authority"; freedom to make professional decisions according to their
own trained judgment rather than according to the dictates of
superiors in a bureaucratic hierarchy.[2] Taking this functional

---

[1] A. M. Henderson and Talcott Parsons (trans.), Max
Weber: The Theory of Social and Economic Organization, p. 331.

[2] Logan Wilson, op. cit., p. 73. This type of authority
has also been described as "expert," "professional," or "functional"; see Henry G. Metcalf and L. Urwick (eds.), Dynamic Administration: The Collected Papers of Mary Parker Follett (New
York: Harper, 1940), pp. 277-81; Herbert A. Simon, Administrative Behavior (New York: The Macmillan Co., 1947), pp. 142-46;

requirement into account, Parsons[1] and others[2] have suggested
that a more functionally appropriate type of formal organization for professionals would be egalitarian rather than bureaucratic in nature, and they have pointed to the strains that
presumably would attend departures from organization as a
"company of equals."

What appears to be functionally appropriate does not
necessarily occur, however, and all departures from the egalitarian ideal may not be equally dysfunctional. As a first step
in exploring these possibilities and their implications in a
specific case, this chapter describes the formal organization
of the Comprehensive Care and Teaching Program (CC&TP).

The Comprehensive Care and Teaching Program

The CC&TP came into being in 1951, when The New York
Hospital - Cornell Medical Center sought and received funds from
The Commonwealth Fund to aid in establishing an experimental
program for comprehensive medicine. In 1952 the Program began
full functioning, and at present (1958) it continues in

Talcott Parsons, Essays in Sociological Theory: Pure and
Applied (Glencoe, Ill.: The Free Press, 1949), pp. 189-91.
        These terms emphasize the basis for authority, while
"individual authority" emphasizes the locus and thus allows for
the possibility that experts may be qualified to make independent decisions but may nevertheless not be allowed to do so
under certain circumstances.

[1]A. M. Henderson and Talcott Parsons, op. cit., p. 60.

[2]Logan Wilson, loc. cit.; Walter I. Wardwell, "Social
Integration, Bureaucratization, and the Professions," Social
Forces, Vol. 33, No. 4 (May, 1955), pp. 356-59.

operation. A teaching and service unit in a large Medical Center, the Program was designed by professionals primarily for professionals; doctors, nurses, social workers, and other ancillary personnel composed the staff. Because the planners were professionals, it might be expected that they would give maximum consideration to the work requirements of the professionals involved and that this would be apparent in the organization of the Program's staff. That is, on the basis of the preceding analysis, a non-bureaucratic, relatively egalitarian structure might be anticipated, particularly with respect to physicians. Because the participants were largely professionals, such a structure would presumably be maintained over time.

As will be seen in this chapter, the official staff organization as it existed initially and as it developed over a five-year period does not, in general, bear out these anticipations. Close examination of the role expectations, unofficial understandings, and actual behavior of physicians in the group, however, reveals a different and more complicated picture, as later chapters will show.

Impetus for Organization of the Program

The initial form which the Program took and the purposes it was designed to achieve stemmed directly from internal dissatisfaction with existing arrangements for fourth-year teaching and out-patient care in the Medical Center. A summary of these arrangements and the reasons for dissatisfaction which

faculty members advanced may therefore serve as a prologue to
description of the Program's organization.[1]

Fourth-Year Teaching

In 1950 and earlier, the course of training for fourth-
year medical students at Cornell University Medical College
consisted of five eight-week sessions, each devoted to study
and practice in different clinical specialties: (1) medicine;
(2) surgery; (3) pediatrics, psychiatry, and part-time elective
subjects; (4) obstetrics and gynecology; and (5) a full-time
elective subject. Students spent the time given to medicine,
pediatrics, and psychiatry largely in the out-patient clinics
attached to these departments. Here, under the supervision of
physicians who held joint appointments in the Hospital as attending physicians and in the Medical College as faculty members, students served as junior physicians; in this capacity
they examined and treated ambulant patients who came to the
clinics for help.

Some members of the faculty, particularly in the
Department of Medicine, viewed the opportunities for learning

[1]For details see the following articles by George G.
Reader: "Comprehensive Medical Care," Journal of Medical Educa-
tion, Vol. 28, No. 7 (July, 1953), pp. 34-40; "Organization and
Development of a Comprehensive Care Program," American Journal
of Public Health, Vol. 44, No. 6 (June, 1954), pp. 760-65; "The
Cornell Comprehensive Care and Teaching Program," in Robert K.
Merton, George G. Reader, and Patricia L. Kendall, op. cit.,
pp. 81-101. See also David P. Barr, "The Teaching of Preven-
tive Medicine," Journal of Medical Education, Vol. 28, No. 3
(March, 1953), pp. 49-56, and by the same author, "Extramural
Facilities in Medical Education," Journal of Medical Education,
Vol. 28, No. 7 (July, 1953), pp. 9-12.

afforded to students under this arrangement as unduly limited. An important part of students' training in the care of ambulant patients, they believed, occurs when they can follow patients and their illnesses over a substantial period of time, sufficient to allow first-hand observation of the course of disease and, simultaneously, to permit supervised experience in long-term relationships between doctor and patient. Eight weeks appeared to provide little opportunity for these continuing observations and contacts; in the General Medical Clinic, for example, students rarely saw the same patient more than once. Faculty members were also concerned over the possibility that short-term contacts between student-physicians and patients contributed to a conception of patients which they had observed to be relatively prevalent among fourth-year students: a tendency to see patients primarily as "disease entities" and "cases." This view they contrasted unfavorably with seeing the patient "as a person," a broader approach which takes into account not only the strictly organic, "medical" condition of the patient, but in addition, his social and psychological situation as this may bear on his illness.

In addition to viewing the brief amount of time students spent in each clinic as a limitation on the educational opportunities offered to students, faculty members perceived another sort of limitation. On the clinic staffs there were virtually no physician-instructors who were salaried, full-time teachers; almost all of the physicians who supervised the work

of students in the clinics were private practitioners who
served without remuneration only one or two half-days each
week. Under this arrangement there was little provision for
maintaining uniformly high standards of teaching, and even less
provision for integrating the educational efforts made by the
various instructors. Moreover, even though the range of problems presented by patients in a given clinic frequently tran-
scended the specialty represented in the clinic, consultants
from other specialties were not easily available to give students the benefit of their teaching and advice. Consequently,
whether students received an adequate and balanced experience
while in the clinics appeared problematical to some observers.

Out-Patient Care

Unfavorable implications for the quality of medical
care which patients received in the clinics were also drawn
from the circumstances noted. Short-term contacts between
student-physician and patient meant discontinuous medical care
for patients who needed to return to the clinics periodically;
each time they came they were likely to see a doctor who was a
stranger to them and to their problems. The absence of a
"core" staff of full-time clinical instructors meant that overall supervision of the standards of medical care provided in
the clinics was largely lacking, and thus, that any particular
patient might or might not receive the best possible care.
Moreover, not having specialty consultants easily available to
physicians in a given clinic resulted in frequent referral of

patients from clinic to clinic. For some observers, this implied that such patients might well be receiving segmental
rather than complete medical care; it also meant that patients
often had to attend two or more different clinics on different
days of the week, a procedure which usually involved inconven-
ience and sometimes hardship for them.

There was dissatisfaction, too, with other aspects of
out-patient care not as closely connected with teaching. Primary among these was the absence of an appointment system for
patients in some clinics. On the one hand this resulted in un-
predictable patient loads from day to day in the clinics. On
the other hand, it gave patients no choice but to wait -- sometimes for hours -- before their turn came to be seen by a
doctor.

Rationale for Change: Comprehensive Care

The positive values underlying these various dissatis-
factions with out-patient teaching and care in the Medical
Center as of 1950 are summed up in the concept of "comprehensive medical care." One spokesman in the Medical College expressed the meaning of this concept as follows:

> ...comprehensive medical care is basically the
> preservation of health and the prevention as well
> as the cure of disease. In practice this implies
> attention to emotional and psychiatric as well as
> physical factors, and continuing supervision of
> the patient in clinic, hospital, or home for a
> sufficient period of time to bring him through
> convalescence and rehabilitation to an optimal
> state of health and productivity, and to maintain
> him in it. Comprehensive care also implies com-
> passionate care; human consideration for the

> patient as a person. It solicits his cooperation
> and imparts to him a willingness to help without
> invading his rights as an individual.[1]

Those faculty members who advocated comprehensive medicine were committed to the belief that, in principle at least, patients deserve to receive this kind of complete, continuous, and compassionate medical care from their doctors. Further, they believed that doctors ideally should learn to give such care while they are medical students.

But they did not know how adequately these beliefs could be translated into practice. As a leading faculty proponent of comprehensive medicine noted, "There exist no adequate patterns for the performance of such a service....Its goal may be fostered by discussion and precepts, but its feasibility can be determined only by extended trial."[2]

Convinced that the Medical Center would be a desirable site for the "extended trial" of comprehensive medical care and teaching which had been suggested, a small group of especially interested faculty members were instrumental in planning and establishing such a program: the CC&TP. So far as possible, in their general plan they tried to correct the defects they had observed in out-patient care and teaching, and to design a unit which would benefit both patients and medical students. By

---

[1] George G. Reader, "Comprehensive Medical Care," pp. 34-35.

[2] David P. Barr, "The Teaching of Preventive Medicine," p. 51.

June 1952 the basic organizational decisions had been made and
approved; they and the modifications in organization which had
occurred after five years of operation are reported in the
remainder of this chapter.

Initial Organization: 1952

Participation of Students

To allow students more extended experience in caring
for patients, the Executive Faculty of the Medical College
voted to lengthen and divide the fourth-year curriculum into
two semesters of 22 1/2 weeks each. They further rearranged
the curriculum so that clinical work in Medicine, Pediatrics,
and Psychiatry formed a single, semester-long "Course in Comprehensive Medicine." During each semester, some forty students -- half of the fourth-year class -- took this course
while the other half studied Surgery, Obstetrics and Gynecology,
and an elective subject in rotation.

While enrolled in the six-month Course in Comprehensive
Medicine (which the CC&TP staff planned and directed), students
spent two half-days each week seeing patients in the General
Medical Clinic. During three of the months they spent an additional two half-days each week seeing patients in the Pediatrics Out-Patient Department, and during the other three
months they devoted an equal period of time to seeing patients
in the Psychiatric Out-Patient Department. Remaining time
during the six-month period was allocated to briefer periods of

study and experience in elective specialties (e.g., dermatology, cardiology), to regular participation in seminars conducted by CC&TP staff members, and to attendance at scheduled conferences and lectures.[1]

Locus of Activities

Selected as the most suitable locus of Program activities and designated "Comprehensive Care Clinics" were the General Medical Clinic and the General Pediatric Clinic. Both Clinics were on-going units in the Hospital with staffs of doctors, nurses, and other ancillary personnel who regularly served large numbers of ambulant patients. In 1952, for example, those in the General Medical Clinic cared for some three thousand patients who made a total of nearly fifteen thousand visits; those in the General Pediatric Clinic cared for approximately twenty-seven hundred patients who made over sixteen thousand visits.[2]

Sponsorship and Personnel

While the Clinics themselves were not new, with the advent of the CC&TP they came under new auspices and acquired additional personnel.

In order to "emphasize the integration necessary to the

----

[1] For elaboration of the nature of these activities, see George G. Reader, "Comprehensive Medical Care," and "Some of the Problems and Satisfactions of Teaching Comprehensive Medicine," Journal of Medical Education, Vol. 31, No. 8 (August, 1956), pp. 544-52.

[2] The Society of the New York Hospital: Annual Report for the Year 1953, p. 69.

practice of comprehensive care,"[1] the CC&TP was conceived as a
nondepartmental unit of the Medical Center as a whole. As
such, the Program became the ultimate responsibility of the
group who made policy for the Medical Center: the Joint Administrative Board. This group appointed a CC&TP Advisory Committee composed of the heads of the Clinical Departments (Medicine,
Surgery, Obstetrics and Gynecology, Psychiatry, Pediatrics),[2]
the Professor of Preventive Medicine, the Director of Social
Service, the Chairman of the Out-Patient Department Committee
of the Medical Board, the Director of the Hospital, the Dean of
the Medical College, the Dean of the Nursing School, and the
Director of the Joint Administrative Board of the Medical
Center. Elected as Chairman of the Committee by its members
was the head of the Department of Medicine.

Members of the Advisory Committee were directly responsible for determining general CC&TP policy and for appointing Program personnel. They first appointed an internist as
Acting Director of the Program, another internist as Resident
to assist him, a Social Service worker, and a Public Health
nurse. By the time the Program began full functioning several
months later, they had changed the title of Acting Director to

---

[1] George G. Reader, "Comprehensive Medical Care," p. 35.

[2] The doctors who serve as heads of the Clinical Departments in the Medical College also hold the position of Chief of
the corresponding Clinical Service in the Hospital. For example, the head of the Department of Medicine in the College is
Physician-in-Chief of the Hospital; the head of the Department
of Surgery is Surgeon-in-Chief, and so on.

Director, and they had created and filled additional salaried
positions so that the roster of personnel appointed especially
for the Program was as follows:

Physicians

Director (full-time; internist)
Assistant Director for Medicine (full-time;
    internist)
Assistant Director for Pediatrics (full-time;
    pediatrician)
Resident in Medicine (full-time; internist)

Consultant in Surgery (half-time)
Consultant in Obstetrics and Gynecology (half-time)
Consultant in Psychiatry (half-time)
Consultant in Preventive Medicine (half-time)

Ancillary Medical Personnel

Public Health Nurse (full-time)
Social Worker (full-time)

Other Personnel

Statistician (one-third-time)

Secretary to the Director (full-time)
Secretary to the Staff (full-time)

In addition to holding positions in the Program, all of the
medical personnel listed above -- doctors, nurse, and social
worker -- were members of appropriate departments in the larger
organizations which composed the Medical Center. For the physicians, this meant that they were on the staffs of both the
Hospital and the Medical College: the internists in the Department of Medicine, the pediatrician in the Department of Pediatrics, the Surgical Consultant in the Department of Surgery,
etc. The Public Health Nurse was a member of the Out-Patient
Department Nursing staff of the Hospital and, simultaneously,

an instructor in the Nursing School; the Social Worker belonged
to the Social Service Department of the Hospital.

Through these various affiliations, almost all of the
newly-appointed Program personnel were formally integrated with
already-existing functional divisions among personnel in the
two Comprehensive Care Clinics and in the Medical Center. An
exception was the statistician who, in a research capacity, was
affiliated solely with the Program.

Supervisory Responsibility

The titles given to the several doctors suggest that
they did not all enter the Clinics and the Program at the same
hierarchical level, with equal responsibilities for administration and supervision. The 1952 organizational plan of the
Program shown in Figure 1 makes the existence of a formal hierarchy explicit, and an official statement[1] amplifies the distinctions shown.

According to the statement, the Director was responsible
to the Advisory Committee for "overall supervision and coordination of the Program," and "ultimately responsible to the
clinical department heads for the care the patients receive";
he was to bring to the Committee "questions of policy" and to
keep them "informed of general progress."[2]

Placed in charge of the General Medical Clinic, the

---

[1] George G. Reader, "Organization and Development of a
Comprehensive Care Program."

[2] Ibid., p. 763.

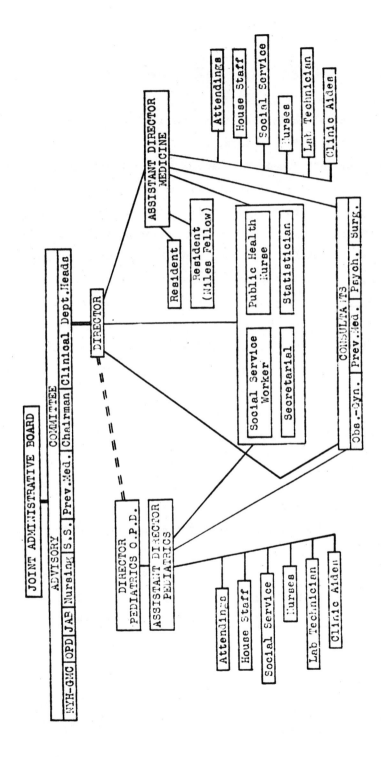

FIGURE 1

ORGANIZATIONAL PLAN OF THE COMPREHENSIVE CARE AND TEACHING PROGRAM: 1952

Assistant Director for Medicine became "responsible to the
Director for the care of all adult patients under the Program
and for students' activities in the Medical Clinic and on
visits to the home."[1] In turn, all of the doctors who taught
and cared for patients in the Medical Clinic were held formally
responsible for these activities to the Assistant Director;
this group of doctors included the Resident in Medicine, a
Fellow in Medicine who had elected to serve as a full-time
Resident in the Clinic, the four specialty consultants, and
some fifty internists who had been serving in the Clinic on a
part-time, unsalaried basis before the CC&TP began and who continued to do so under the new arrangement. Also responsible to
the Assistant Director for Medicine -- as well as to their
immediate superiors in their respective departments -- were the
newly-appointed Public Health Nurse, the Social Service Worker,
and the other ancillary personnel who had been in the Clinic
before the Program began: two nurses, a Nursing Aide, two
Clinic Aides (clerk-receptionists), and a Laboratory Technician.
While students were in the Medical Clinic, they were viewed as
junior physicians, responsible to the individual doctors who
served as their instructors and to those in charge of the
Program.

Since the Pediatric Clinic was already under the charge
of a full-time Out-Patient Department Clinical Director who was

[1] Ibid.

not officially on the CC&TP staff (though she worked closely
with it), the Assistant Director for Pediatrics did not have
responsibilities that exactly paralleled those of her counterpart in Medicine. In Pediatrics, the Assistant Director was to
maintain "liaison" and to be "responsible with the pediatric
OPD director for the teaching activities in the General Pediatric Clinic and on home visits to pediatric patients."[1] To
the extent that she shared such teaching responsibility, the
activities of some thirty unsalaried pediatricians who cared
for patients and taught part-time in the Pediatric Clinic came
under her purview, as did those of the four specialty consultants (who served both Medical and Pediatric Clinics). Ancillary personnel in the Pediatric Clinic were responsible to the
Clinical Director rather than to the Assistant Director. As in
the Medical Clinic, in their capacity as junior physicians
medical students were answerable to their individual instructors and to those in charge of the Program.

Thus the Advisory Committee not only augmented the professional medical staffs of the two Clinics when they appointed
a small number of physicians to serve there on salaried full-
time and half-time bases. Through designating a Director and
two Assistant Directors within this group and assigning to them
graded supervisory responsibilities, the Advisory Committee
introduced a new formal hierarchy of authority among physicians

[1] Ibid.

in the Clinics. What this formal hierarchy of authority meant
to physicians in terms of their day-to-day actions and expectations will be discussed in following chapters. Here, however,
two significant facts may be noted.

First, the hierarchical principle had ample precedent
in the Medical Center. Physicians who receive advanced training while on the House Staff of the Hospital are traditionally
organized in hierarchical fashion: within each Clinical Service,
interns are responsible to assistant residents, assistant residents to head resident, and head resident to the Chief of the
Service. Correlatively, each higher level is responsible for
and supervises the work of the level below. Moreover, even
before the CC&TP there were lines of authority in the two
Clinics under discussion. As indicated, the Pediatric Clinic
already had a full-time Clinical Director who was answerable to
the Pediatrician-in-Chief for patient care and teaching in the
Clinic. And while the Medical Clinic had not had a full-time
Director, it had been under the charge of a part-time attending
physician who was responsible for its operation to the Physician-in-Chief of the Hospital.

Second, although the Advisory Committee specified a new
hierarchy of authority in the Clinics, they did not give those
in Charge any major sanctioning powers, either positive or
negative. That is, they retained the right to appoint, dismiss,
and promote physicians in the Program. In this respect they
also followed precedent in the Medical Center, where these

rights are traditional prerogatives of the Chief of each Service. (Appointments, promotions, and dismissals on the Hospital staff are officially made by the Board of Governors of the Hospital on the basis of recommendations offered by the Chief of a Service and approved by the Medical Board; in the Medical College, the Board of Trustees of Cornell University acts officially on the basis of recommendations made by the Head of a Department and approved by the Executive Faculty of the College.)

Later Developments in Organization: 1957

Figure 2 presents the organizational plan of the CC&TP as of 1957. Comparison of this plan with the plan of 1952 shown in Figure 1 indicates that after five years of operation the Program retained much of its initial structure. The Joint Administrative Board of the Medical Center still sponsored the unit, the composition of the Advisory Committee and its relationship to the staff remained the same, and most of the original positions on the staff level continued to exist (Director, Assistant Director for Medicine, Assistant Director for Pediatrics, four specialty Consultants, two Secretaries). However, alterations are also apparent. The number of salaried staff members had increased, as had the number within this group with titles indicative of administrative and supervisory responsibilities. Correlatively, some embryonic functional divisions had developed further and become explicitly recognized.

More specifically, it will be recalled that the Program originally had thirteen salaried positions. Five years later,

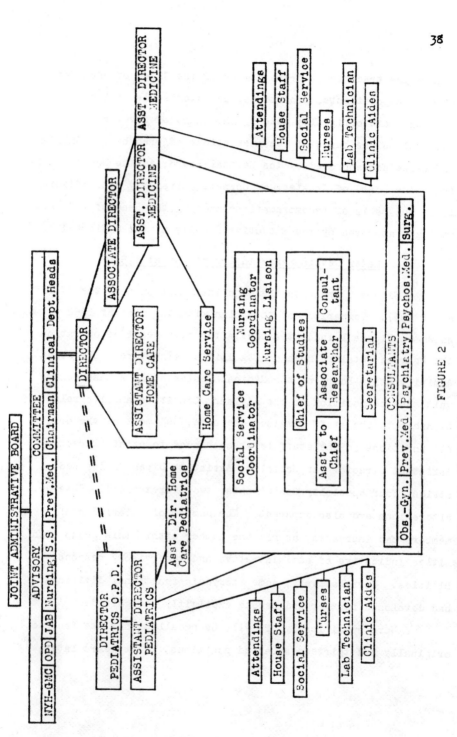

FIGURE 2

ORGANIZATIONAL PLAN OF THE COMPREHENSIVE CARE AND TEACHING PROGRAM: 1957

as the following list[1] indicates, there were twenty-eight such positions.

Physicians

Director (full-time; internist)
**Associate Director (full-time; internist)

Asst. Director for Medicine (half-time; internist)
**Asst. Director for Medicine (half-time; internist)
Asst. Director for Pediatrics (full-time; pediatrician)
**Asst. Director for Home Care (half-time; internist)
**Asst. Director for Home Care in Pediatrics (full-time; pediatrician)

Asst. Resident in Medicine (full-time; internist; rotating)
*Asst. Resident in Medicine (full-time; internist; rotating)
*Asst. Resident in Medicine (full-time; internist; rotating)
*Asst. Resident in Medicine (full-time; internist; rotating)

Consultant in Surgery (half-time)
Consultant in Obstetrics and Gynecology (half-time)
Consultant in Psychiatry (half-time)
*Consultant in Psychiatry (half-time)
*Consultant in Child Psychiatry (half-time)
Consultant in Preventive Medicine - Rehabilitation (half-time)

Ancillary Medical Personnel

Nursing Coordinator (full-time)
**Nurse for Liaison (full-time)

Social Service Coordinator (full-time)

*Laboratory Technician (full-time)

Other Personnel

**Chief of Studies (full-time; sociologist)

---

[1]A single asterisk (*) indicates that the position was added after 1952; a double asterisk indicates that the new position carried supervisory responsibilities.

*Associate Researcher (full-time; sociologist)
Assistant to Chief of Studies (half-time;
    sociologist)

*Consultant in Sociology (full-time)

Secretary to the Director (full-time)
Secretary to the Staff (full-time)
*Secretary for Home Care (full-time)

The total number of positions had more than doubled, and as
this list shows, the number of supervisory positions had increased from three in 1952 to eleven by 1957.

Of the eight apparently new supervisory positions, two
in fact represented "old" positions which had been renamed
during the Program's first year so as to accord more closely
with the actual activities of the persons who held them; the
Public Health Nurse in the original list became the Nursing
Coordinator of the later list, and the Social Worker became the
Social Service Coordinator. A third position -- Assistant
Director for Medicine -- was also "old" in the sense that the
title had existed initially; it was new, however, in that the
original full-time position had been split into two half-time
positions in order to retain valued staff members who wished to
devote some of their time to private practice.

The remaining five supervisory positions were entirely
new. Four had been created in the course of expanding the
focus of CC&TP activities, specifically, home care and research.
When, during the Program's third year, the decision was reached
to provide more students with planned experiences in home care
by enlarging the Home Care Service for patients, the positions

of Assistant Director for Home Care and Assistant Director for
Home Care in Pediatrics came into being. With the intensifica-
tion of interest in research in patient care that also took
place during the Program's third year, the position of Chief of
Studies was created (as well as the other non-supervisory research positions listed). Concern with improving continuity of
care between out-patient and in-patient services in the Hospital led to creation of the position of Liaison Nurse during
that same year.

Linked as they were to newly emphasized activities and
aims, none of these four positions involved lengthening the
number of supervisory levels in the Program. That is, they
represented further "horizontal" division of labor rather than
"vertical" expansion. This was not the case with the final and
most recently added position: Associate Director of the CC&TP.
Specifically in charge of the entire teaching program in Medicine, the Associate Director was responsible to the Director.
As the organizational plan in Figure 2 indicates, the Assistant
Directors for Medicine thereupon became responsible to the
Associate Director as well as to the Director of the Program.
In essence, then, introducing the position of Associate Direc-
tor added another level to the hierarchy of supervision in the
Program; over the five-year period, vertical as well as hori-
zontal expansion had occurred.

A Note on Conditions Facilitating Innovation and Change

It is beyond the scope of this report to provide a

detailed analysis of the decision-making processes involved in creating and changing the CC&TP.[1] Attention should be called, however, to two general conditions that apparently served to facilitate positive decisions about both innovation and change throughout the development of the Program.

One of these conditions was the initial and continued availability of "outside" funds from a foundation. Faculty members who advocated a program of comprehensive care were aware from the beginning that existing budgetary allotments in the Medical Center would not cover the necessary new expenditures for salaries of full-time staff members. Without additional funds, any large-scale effort to innovate -- whatever its intrinsic worth -- would thus meet with understandable resistance from departments whose financial resources were already committed elsewhere. Before formally proposing the curriculum changes entailed in the CC&TP to the Executive Faculty of the Medical College, therefore, the planners obtained a substantial three-year grant from The Commonwealth Fund to support the Program on an experimental basis. This grant permitted the Executive Faculty to judge the potential merits of the proposed curriculum changes impartially, without regard for the inroads that their approval might make on their respective departmental

---

[1] The process of organizational change is, however, the central analytic focus of another report that covers the first year of the Program's operation. See M. E. W. Goss, "Change in the Cornell Comprehensive Care and Teaching Program," in R. K. Merton, G. G. Reader, and P. L. Kendall, op. cit., pp. 249-70.

budgets. Later, when the Program was formally established, the
funds allotted the Program provided latitude for changes that
would have been impossible had there been competition for
scarce departmental funds. In particular, the decision, in
1954, to expand staff and activities could not have taken place
without the additional financial support provided by a second
three-year grant from The Commonwealth Fund; at that time
neither the Medical College nor the Hospital was ready to
finance the expansion of the CC&TP, however desirable or necessary this might appear to participants in the Program.

The leverage for organizational innovation was thus
supplied by an institution whose function it is to counteract
financial, and, in principle, irrelevant resistances to innovation. In this particular sense, then, foundations can be regarded as an institutional device for facilitating social in-
ventions in other institutions.

A second condition was the definition of the Program,
from the beginning, as an experimental enterprise. It was
oriented toward change, rather than having change regarded as
a sign of defeat. Since the outlook of the planners as well as
of others in the Medical Center was frankly experimental, every
aspect of the CC&TP was initially regarded as being on trial.
Organizational change was equated with potential improvement.[1]
The outlook of those in the Program remained experimental,

---

[1]The equation of change with improvement is discussed
in greater detail by Goss, ibid., pp. 257-58.

although the particular features of the Program considered to be on trial gradually changed. As certain components of the Program seemed to prove their worth, they were taken to justify continuance as integral features of the organization. The CC&TP staff and the Advisory Committee then transferred their experimental attitudes to objectives and activities that had originally been less clearly outlined. Notable among these was the experience of students with the home care of patients and research by the staff on problems in patient care.

Even when foundations remove financial barriers, of course, institutional innovation is not inevitable. For effective innovation, there must also be a climate of values that favors or at least tolerates change and experiment. Such a climate clearly characterized the Medical Center. More generally, change and experiment directed toward improving the care of the sick are an honored part of the tradition of medicine. As the guardians of that tradition, medical schools are committed to exploring new arrangements, and thus can be expected to welcome organizational innovation more readily than would institutions with other values.[1]

Under such conditions, it is less remarkable that the Program changed as it did than that its organizational structure remained stable throughout the five-year period. Even

[1] For further discussion of this matter, see Robert K. Merton, "Some Preliminaries to a Sociology of Medical Education," in R. K. Merton, G. G. Reader, and P. L. Kendall, op. cit., pp. 3-79, at pp. 5-7.

before the Program began, hierarchical organization was nothing
new for physicians in the clinics. And as the Program expanded,
extension of the hierarchical principle to cover new positions
seemed to be largely taken for granted. The later structure
was only a more elaborate version of the earlier one rather
than a radically different and more egalitarian form.

Summary and Discussion

The official hierarchy of supervision apparent in the
initial organization of the CC&TP was deliberately instituted
by a committee of responsible professionals in order to improve
existing conditions and aid achievement of Program objectives.
In succeeding years of the Program's operation the hierarchy
was not only maintained but accentuated. Thus as various activities received greater emphasis, personnel were added and
appropriate supervisory positions on already-existing levels
were created; as the total number of activities and personnel
increased, an additional level of supervision was introduced.

This manifest adherence to the hierarchical principle
of organization requires explanation in view of the fact that a
large proportion of the persons who participated in the Program
were professional physicians. As suggested in the introductory
section, professionals require "individual authority" if they
are to carry out their work properly; accordingly, organization
along egalitarian rather than hierarchical lines might have
been expected. An obvious and immediate explanation for what
occurred is of course contained in one of the conditions which

the Program was specifically designed to improve: the relative
paucity of full-time supervision and coordination of patient
care and teaching activities in the clinics. In principle at
least, the CC&TP Advisory Committee achieved the desired improvement by appointing a small number of physicians who would
serve on a full-time salaried basis, and assigning to them
graded responsibilities for overseeing as well as participating
directly in the activities. In this sense, the official hierarchical structure of the CC&TP came about and was maintained
because it was required for the attainment of organizational
objectives: initially, improvement of teaching and patient care,
and later, research as well.

　　　　Less obvious but even more to the point, however, is the
outlook which planners (and participants) of the Program had.
As the next chapter will suggest more fully, for them there was
no serious contradiction between introducing a supervisory hierarchy and preserving the additional authority of physicians in
the Program; hierarchies of supervision among physicians were
not unusual in the Hospital and there were fairly clear professional norms for conduct in such relationships. The planners
and participants could generally take for granted that physicians
in supervisory positions would carry out their responsibilities
in ways which were professionally approved, and therefore that
the norms and values of the profession regarding supervision and
the rights of the individual physician would be upheld. What
these norms and values were, and how doctors applied them to
various clinical situations will be examined in the following
chapter.

CHAPTER III

INFLUENCE AND AUTHORITY AMONG PHYSICIANS

Hierarchical organization may, but need not, mean cur-
tailment of the individual authority of professionals. In
analyzing how professionals may preserve individual authority
within the framework of hierarchical organization, a useful
beginning is provided by existing theoretical analyses and
empirical studies of supervisory relationships that involve
primarily non-professional personnel. As Gouldner,[1] Blau,[2]
and others[3] have observed in various contexts, those who hold
superordinate positions in an official hierarchy may have the
formal right to impose their decisions upon subordinates (that
is, to exercise authority), but in fact they do not always
choose to do so. Instead, they may attempt to exert influence
in the desired direction through education, persuasion, or

---

[1]Alvin W. Gouldner, op. cit., pp. 215-28.

[2]Peter M. Blau, The Dynamics of Bureaucracy, pp. 161-79.

[3]Herbert A. Simon, Administrative Behavior (New York:
Macmillan Co., 1947), pp. 11-16 and 123-46; Chester I. Barnard,
The Functions of the Executive (Cambridge: Harvard University
Press, 1938), pp. 161-84; Henry C. Metcalf and L. Urwick (eds.),
The Collected Papers of Mary Parker Follett (New York: Harper,
1940), pp. 247-94; Robert K. Merton, Social Theory and Social
Structure, pp. 339-40; Reinhard Bendix, "Bureaucracy: the
Problem and its Setting," American Sociological Review, Vol.
12, No. 5 (October, 1947), pp. 493-507.

advice. Further, selection of one or another of these potential modes of control is rarely a simple function of the
personal preference of the persons in charge. It is becoming
increasingly clear that if they are to discharge their responsibilities effectively, in some measure they are socially
constrained to take notice of the relevant norms and values of
subordinates and to act accordingly. Through being incorpo-
rated in role expectations which specify appropriate behavior
patterns for supervisory relationships under various circumstances, these norms and values may set the real limits -- in
contrast with "official" limits -- on the kinds of supervisory
control that will be feasible in particular work situations.

As this chapter will show, supervisory relationships
among physicians offer an extreme -- and therefore instruc-
tive -- example of the operation of this general principle.
These relationships also offer suggestive evidence concerning
how hierarchical organization of professionals may exist, as in
the CC&TP, and yet be reconciled with maintenance of individual
authority for each professional. Toward these ends, the types
of supervisory control which were institutionalized among physicians in the CC&TP are first illustrated and described in the
chapter. Then the relationship between type of control and
sphere of work is examined, and for each sphere both observed
behavior and underlying norms and values are reported.

Types of Supervisory Control

Physicians in the CC&TP recognized and distinguished between two major types of supervisory prerogatives: the right to make decisions and the right to give advice.[1] Examination of their opinions and behavior in several instances which involved supervision may serve as a basis for subsequent analysis of the general nature of the two types of prerogatives.

Case I: Scheduling

For each session of the General Medical Clinic, the physician in charge made out and posted a master schedule in which physician-instructors were paired with students and assigned patients and examining rooms. When physicians arrived at the Clinic each morning or afternoon, they customarily consulted the master schedule to find out which patients they would be seeing that day and where, and to find out which students' work they would be called upon to check. "Checking" students was the main teaching activity of physicians in the Clinic and it customarily took place in the following manner: after a student had finished interviewing and examining his assigned patient, he reported the findings to his assigned physician-instructor, who first discussed with the student alternative probable diagnoses, possible plans for therapy, and the

---

[1] As a later section of this chapter will indicate in detail, supervision in the administrative realm generally involved the right to make decisions; supervision in professional realms of activity, however, entailed only the right to give advice.

nature of the particular disease that seemed to be involved;
then the physician-instructor proceeded to examine the patient
briefly himself. Finally he conferred again with the student
concerning what should be done next for the patient, and he
countersigned the notes which the student had written in the
patient's chart.

Occasionally a physician expressed a preference for
continuing to check a particular student, usually because he
had found that the student provided him with an especially
gratifying teaching experience. When this occurred the physician in charge tried to take the preference into account in
making future assignments though, as both he and the other
Clinic physicians understood, to do so was not always possible
within the framework of the sometimes disparate schedules of
students and physicians. There were also times when the physician assigned to a student was unavailable when that student
was ready to be checked.[1] In such instances the physician was
known or assumed to be occupied elsewhere with unexpected

---

[1] However, most students considered the doctors assigned
to them "almost always" or "usually" available when needed.
More particularly, four out of the five classes of medical students who participated in the CC&TP during the period
covered by this report were asked the following question: "Were
the attending doctors assigned to you in the Comprehensive Care
Clinics easily available when you needed them?" Of the 337
students, 17 per cent checked "almost always"; 55 per cent
checked "usually"; 26 per cent checked "rarely"; and two per
cent did not answer the question. See "Master Card Codebook
for the First Eight Groups to Go Through the Cornell Comprehensive Care and Teaching Program: Classes of 1953 - 1956," Prepared by the Bureau of Applied Social Research, Columbia University (November, 1956), p. 51. (Dittoed.)

teaching or patient care duties, and the physician in charge
either found a substitute or checked the student himself.[1]

But for the most part, physicians complied as a matter
of course with the directives contained in the schedule, and
seemed to take for granted the right of the physician in charge
of the Clinic to make decisions about these routine aspects of
their work. Specific formal penalties for non-compliance did
not exist, nor did they appear necessary to physicians. "Of
course the Clinic needs a schedule," an attending physician remarked, "and naturally we try to follow it. Otherwise the
Clinic would fall apart."

In this case, physicians were not particularly apt to
review critically each decision made by the physician in
charge; they tended to accept the scheduling directives without
much question and their compliance appeared to be relatively
automatic. There were other occasions, however, when they
carefully examined the content of a request before they decided
to comply with it.

Case II: Visit Reports

On one such occasion, the Director of the CC&TP asked
both of the Residents to fill out visit reports for a week on a
trial basis. These reports were designed for eventual use by
students in recording contacts with patients, but before dis-
tributing them to students the Director wanted to know how some

[1]For a more general discussion of this type of situation see infra, section entitled "Administration."

physicians as well as the student-representatives would react
to using the form. He selected the Residents rather than the
Assistant Directors of the CC&TP or the attending physicians on
the part-time staff because, as junior members of the full-time
staff, the Residents had fewer fixed responsibilities and more
available time.

The Residents clearly objected to the request: "You
mean you want us to fill out those forms too?" said one with
some surprise. And the other added, "We have more important
things to do than that." The Director replied, "Yes, I mean
you. We need your opinions before we decide the form is ready
for the students." The Residents said no more, though they did
not appear to be convinced.

Nevertheless, at the end of the week they turned in
their completed visit reports in accordance with the Director's
request. They had reviewed the content of the request and they
disapproved of it. "I think it's a waste of time, but he's the
boss," commented one of the Residents during the week. In
spite of the absence of any direct, formal penalty for non-
compliance, the Residents were not eager to alienate the Director or to have him believe they were uncooperative; upon com-
pletion of their residencies they knew they would have to
depend partly on his good opinion to obtain desirable posts.
Thus they complied, and in doing so they recognized the higher
status of the Director as well as his right to make such
requests.

Case III: Preceptor Switch

Rather than result in the reluctant compliance which the Residents displayed in filling out visit reports, critical review of a request often led to approval and consequently, to more willing compliance. This is what happened when the Director asked the preceptors -- two internists and two pediatricians -- to switch their groups of students at midsemester, so that each group might benefit from the guidance of both pediatrician and internist while they were in the Program. The Director had earlier discussed with the preceptors the possibility of switching groups, and they had agreed then that this would probably be desirable if it could be arranged. One of the preceptors noted:

> I think that would be sensible, since students
> really should be exposed to both orientations,
> and it would also give us a chance to get to
> know more of the students during the term.

Thus they welcomed the Director's later formal request and they quite willingly traded their respective groups of students at midsemester.

In spite of their enthusiasm for the plan, if the preceptors had not been authorized to switch groups by the Director they would not have done so. "He's the Director and it's his responsibility, not mine," explained one of the preceptors. Like the Residents in the preceding case, in this instance the preceptors asknowledged the Director's right to make the ultimate decision, regardless of their own personal evaluation of the content.

Case IV: Chart Review

As might be anticipated, physicians were not always
ready to comply with a request irrespective of their own evaluation. In fact, in the case of chart review they were prepared
to comply only if they approved.

When the physician in charge reviewed charts at the
beginning of each Clinic session, he examined the recent notes
made by students and physicians[1] in the charts of patients
scheduled for revisits during the session. If he had comments
on the care a patient was receiving, he wrote them out in the
form of suggestions and clipped them to the chart where they
could be seen by the student or physician with whom the patient
had an appointment. Typical of the suggestions offered were
the following:

-- Suggest basal metabolism and serum cholesterol
   on this patient.

-- No complete urinalysis recorded in past six
   months on this diabetic. How about looking for
   albumin and doubly-refractile bodies?

-- Occult blood in stool suggests need for barium
   enema and proctoscopy.

-- Elderly patient with insomnia may be depressed.
   Psychiatric consultation?

---

[1]All students cared for patients under the supervision
of qualified physicians, but some patients were cared for by
physicians alone. In the latter case, the physicians themselves wrote the notes for the patients' charts; when a student
was also involved in caring for a patient, the student wrote
the notes and his instructor countersigned them, thus signify-
ing approval of the notes as part of the patient's permanent
record.

If, as sometimes happened, the physician in charge had no advice to offer, he simply initialed the chart to indicate that
it had been reviewed.

The Director, who had instituted the procedure,[1] looked
on reviewing charts in this manner as a form of supervision
which in the long run would aid in maintaining high standards
of patient care in the Clinic. He explained: "Going over the
charts regularly lets the doctors know we're following what
they're doing, and that's what counts in keeping standards up."

Apart from what could be learned through examination of
successive entries in the charts themselves, no records were
kept of whether or not physicians actually carried out the suggestions that were offered. However, the physician in charge
believed that compliance with his suggestions occurred more
often than not. Nevertheless, he recognized that compliance
was always problematical; in accordance with the professional
norms and values described more fully in a later section of
this chapter, physicians reserved to themselves the right to
accept or reject the suggestions about patient care which the
physician in charge might make. "I believe a doctor should
always be open to advice about his patients, since no one is
ever so good he can't learn something from others occasionally,"
said an attending physician in the Clinic. However, he

---

[1] While the specific procedure was new to the Clinic,
the principle of review as a means of maintaining standards had
ample precedent in the Hospital, as the following chapter will
indicate in some detail.

continued: "But it's up to the doctor who's actually taking
care of the patient to make the final decisions -- he's the one
who's responsible for the patient, remember."

This view was shared by physicians in the Clinic generally, including those who held supervisory positions. The
Director himself remarked: "If you're reviewing charts you
don't expect the doctors to carry out every suggestion you
make. You may have a good reason for suggesting something
should be done, but they may have a better reason for not doing
it, since they know the patients."

In the case of chart review, then, physicians interpreted the official right to supervise as the right to advise
rather than to make decisions governing their behavior. They
considered it their duty to take supervisory suggestions about
patient care into account, and in this sense they accepted
supervision. But they also felt obliged, as responsible physicians, to examine such suggestions critically, and to follow
them only if they appeared to be in the patients' best interests according to their own professional judgment. Correlatively, they would have considered it a breach of their duty as
physicians to carry out a supervisory suggestion regarding the
care they gave to a patient without independently evaluating
its merits.

As could hardly be otherwise under such conditions,
formal sanctions for non-compliance with supervisory suggestions of this sort were not in evidence. In the very

infrequent instances when a supervising physician believed the
well-being of a patient was seriously threatened by what he
judged to be inadequate medical care, he made a point of discussing the case personally with the responsible physician.
These discussions focused not on the fact that the responsible
physician had failed to follow the suggestions offered, but on
the technical problems presented by the patient, viewed in the
light of current medical knowledge and practice. Alternatively
or concomitantly, the supervising physician might arrange to
have the patient presented by a student at a teaching conference, where the patient's problems and medical care were discussed by students and faculty members, presumably for the
benefit of the students present. In either case, there was a
strong likelihood that the responsible physician would revise
his approach to the patient's care as a result of the discussion, although sometimes it was the supervising physician
himself who became convinced that his suggestions had been less
wise than he had originally thought.

Types of Control

The type of control manifested in chart review clearly
differs in certain respects from that exemplified in scheduling,
reporting patient contacts, or switching preceptor groups. In
each of those cases, a physician who was formally in charge
made a decision which indicated that one particular course of
action was to be followed by other physicians. Whether the
decision was expressed through an impersonal schedule or

through a personal request, it was intended to leave little
margin for alternative behavior on the part of those involved;
compliance was expected. Physicians understood this; in the
three instances described, they believed that in making such
requests the physician in charge was within the rights attached
to the supervisory status he held, and that they had an obligation to behave in accordance with the requests. Corresponding-
ly, and even though in one case they disapproved of the content
of the request, they complied overtly. Thus the process of
control was direct, and its outcome -- overt compliance -- was
relatively predictable.

In chart review, on the other hand, the rights attached
to the status of physician in charge were more limited; consistent with professional norms, he made decisions which he
intended and physicians interpreted as leaving a wide margin
for alternative behavior. Accordingly, the decisions were expressed as suggestions, and overt compliance was expected and
occurred only if the suggestion met with approval after independent critical evaluation. Here the process of control was
indirect, and the outcome of the process was in principle un-
predictable.

Clearly, the latter "indirect" process represents an
institutionalized form of exercising influence; advice was
given which, according to the norms of physicians, might legitimately be rejected by recipients. In contrast, the "direct"
process which was described represents the exercise of

authority; supervisory decisions were made which, however phrased, ordinarily could not be rejected legitimately by those whose actions they concerned.

It should be noted, nevertheless, that both types of control had at least one feature in common: there were neither specific formal penalties for non-compliance nor specific formal rewards for compliance. General formal sanctions existed, of course, in the form of possible promotion within the hierarchy or dismissal from the staff. These sanctions, however, rested mainly with the Chiefs of the Services, and the relationship between their application and performance in the Clinic was far from obvious either to the physicians who worked in the Clinic or to the observer. More obvious was the importance of anticipated informal sanctions, as illustrated with respect to the Residents in the case of visit reports, and with respect to the entire group of physicians in the case of chart review.

Activity, Norms, and Types of Control

The two normatively different types of control -- influence and authority -- were not confined to the four instances described. Each occurred more generally among physicians in the Medical Center, and as this section will indicate, which one was believed appropriate in a particular situation depended immediately upon whether physicians considered the sphere of activity in question to be "administrative" or "professional" in nature, and ultimately, upon the norms and values they held regarding each sphere.

Patient Care

As the account of chart review suggests, physicians believed patient care to be a professional activity which required independence in decision-making, i.e., individual authority for each doctor. Accordingly, supervising physicians generally attempted to exert influence rather than authority when they wished to affect the behavior of other physicians in this realm of activity.

Informal questioning of physicians with supervisory responsibility for patient care in various units of the Hospital indicated that, except in the rare case of an exceptionally stubborn and uninformed intern, they were not prepared to give anything resembling an order to another doctor concerning the care of that doctor's patient. Acknowledging that because they were officially responsible for the professional care given to patients in their units they had the formal right to make such requests, for example, two different supervising physicians independently went on to make almost identical comments: "You just never do it, though," said one of the physicians. "But you don't do it, of course," remarked the other.

Observation of interaction among doctors in the General Medical Clinic bore out these statements, for it revealed no instance in which a supervising physician officially requested a physician on the staff to follow a particular course of action in the care he gave his patient. (Interns did not work in the Clinic, and so there was no opportunity to observe whether they were in fact ever treated differently from residents and attending physicians in this respect.) However, observation did show a great many instances -- apart from chart review -- in which supervising physicians made some form of suggestion to those in the Clinic whose work they were supervising.

Expressions of control of this sort occurred most often in the weekly CC&TP History meetings, which were attended by members of the full-time professional staff and held for the purpose of insuring that Family Care patients were receiving medical attention in accordance with principles of comprehensive care. The Director presided over the meetings, and it was his practice, for each family under consideration, first to inquire about the current medical status of members of that family. After the physician who was taking care of the family had reported recent developments to the group and the Director had looked over the patients' charts, the Director frequently had something to say about one or another aspect of the care being given. The following comments, addressed to the responsible physician in each case, are representative of the many which he made:

> -- You're not going to keep Mrs. B. on this
> amount of digitalis indefinitely, are you?
> I doubt if she needs that much now.

-- Mr. J. doesn't seem to be improving as he
should with serpasil. Maybe you ought to try
apresoline instead.

-- Why don't you see if you can persuade Mrs. K.
to bring her husband with her next time she
comes to the Clinic? Without his cooperation
she'll never be able to get as much rest as
she needs.

-- Before deciding definitely on a management
plan for Mrs. G. I'd have a regitine test run.
That would rule out the possibility of pheo-
chromocytoma, and you don't want to do anything much until you know about that for sure.

-- I think I'd explore the possibility that Mrs.
M.'s attacks are related to her job situation --
she changed jobs not so long ago, didn't she?

The physicians to whom the Director addressed these implicit or
explicit suggestions were his juniors in age, experience, and
formal rank. Yet they felt at liberty to disagree with him and
on occasion they did, countering with their reasons for pro-
ceeding along other lines. A group discussion of the relative
merits of each approach frequently ensued, and although each
person expressed his own opinion and attempted to convince
others on the basis of whatever evidence he could produce, no
one -- including the Director -- insisted categorically that a
particular approach be followed. In every case the final
decision was left up to the physician who was caring for the
patient.

Professional Norms and Values

Underlying and legitimating such behavior in the realm
of patient care were, of course, certain firmly institutionalized values of the medical profession: acceptance of personal

responsibility for patients, together with acknowledgment of
one's own potential limitations in fulfilling that responsibility.[1]

Physicians in the General Medical Clinic did not often
verbalize their beliefs regarding personal responsibility for
patient care. Rather, such personal responsibility appeared to
be a basic premise for behavior, an ultimate value which was so
taken for granted that verbalization was ordinarily superfluous.
By and large, only when physicians found themselves with apparently irreconcilable differences of opinion in discussions about
the diagnosis or treatment of a particular patient were they
likely to express themselves:

-- I still think I'd avoid butazolidine in the
   management of that patient if he were mine.
   Frankly, I've rarely seen a patient with gout
   where butazolidine did much good, and it
   often has harmful side effects.

-- In my judgment, using dicumerol for thrombo-
   phlebitis is asking for trouble, because the
   risk of hemorrhage is too great. But she's
   your patient, and if you're going to go ahead
   with it, what happens is your responsibility.

-- I felt that liver and I don't think it's beyond
   normal limits. Therefore I wouldn't say that
   the problem was liver disease, but more likely
   nephrosis. If I were responsible, I'd get another opinion before making a diagnosis of cirrhosis.

The first of these remarks was made by one attending physician
to another concerning a patient whom they had both seen

[1]For an official, general statement of these values,
see Principles of Medical Ethics (Chicago: American Medical Association, 1957), especially Sections 2, 5, 6, and 8.

presented at a conference; the second, by the Assistant Director for Medicine to one of the CC&TP Residents; and the last, by an attending physician to another attending who had asked his opinion. Each of the remarks explicitly assigns personal responsibility to the physician whose patient was under discussion; implicitly, the remarks affirm the fundamental importance physicians attributed to such assignment, an importance that was daily attested by their behavior.

Assumption of personal responsibility for patients would seem to account in large measure for physicians' unwillingness to take or give authoritative orders concerning patient care. For once this value was accepted -- as it apparently was by physicians in both supervisory and non-supervisory positions -- to give an order meant usurping another doctor's professional responsibility, as well as taking over the ever-present risk of being proved wrong by later events. And to follow an order, if given, without independently evaluating it was equivalent to being irresponsible professionally. Perhaps needless to say, no doctor wanted to be open to either charge -- i.e., to violate these professional norms -- and thus it is not surprising that no orders were given in the first place.

Nevertheless, as has been indicated, physicians were willing to give and accept advice in the area of patient care. The values underlying such behavior found expression in their beliefs regarding the limitations of any single doctor's medical knowledge and skill, and in the significance which they attached to possession of these attributes.

As a survey of the opinions of more than five hundred physicians in the Medical Center indicated, almost all of the doctors queried (97 per cent) believed extensive knowledge of medical facts to be of considerable importance in judging the competence of physicians in their specialty.[1] Moreover, they were virtually unanimous in evaluating skill in the realm of diagnosis as of great importance; fully 94 per cent of the group did so, while five per cent judged this skill to be of moderate importance and less than one per cent thought it of minor importance.[2] But the demonstrably high value which physicians placed upon having medical knowledge and diagnostic skill did not mean they thought they could be individually

---

[1] The survey utilized mailed questionnaires and was conducted by David Caplovitz of the Bureau of Applied Social Research in 1956.

The question on which the above information is based read as follows: "How much importance do you personally attach to extensive knowledge of medical facts when judging the competence of clinical students and physicians in your specialty?" Physicians were requested to check one of four answers -- "great importance," "moderate importance," "minor importance," or "no importance" -- for each of three categories of people: "3rd year student," "4th year student," and "Physician in your specialty."

The exact distribution of answers for the last-named category was as follows: 70 per cent of the 507 physicians assigned extensive knowledge of medical facts "great importance"; 27 per cent assigned it "moderate importance"; two per cent assigned it "minor importance"; and one per cent did not answer the question.

[2] One per cent of the 507 physicians did not answer the question. Except for the substitution of the phrase, "skill in the realm of diagnosis," the question was exactly the same as that cited in the previous footnote.

omniscient in these matters. When asked how they would feel if
a physician in their specialty were to "admit his uncertainties
with respect to a diagnostic problem," only four per cent expressed any degree of disapproval of this behavior, as contrasted with fully 86 per cent who definitely approved of admitting uncertainty when it existed.[1] Apparently they expected
to be uncertain some proportion of the time, and in accordance
with the norms of medical practice they believed in admitting
it.[2]

These evaluations seem to explain at least in part why
physicians would not only tolerate but, on occasion, actually
welcome advice in matters of patient care, even though they
would not consider the possibility of orders. That is, because
they had learned as professionals to place a high value upon

[1] The question read as follows: "How would you feel if a
third year student, fourth year student, and physician in your
specialty were to admit his uncertainties with respect to a
diagnostic problem?" For each of the three categories of
people, physicians were requested to check one of five answers:
"disapprove strongly," "disapprove mildly," "would not care,"
"approve mildly," or "approve strongly."
The exact distribution of their answers for the category, "physicians in your specialty" was as follows: one per
cent said they would "disapprove strongly" if a colleague were
to admit his uncertainties with respect to a diagnostic problem; three per cent would "disapprove mildly"; seven per cent
"would not care"; 16 per cent would "approve mildly"; 71 per
cent would "approve strongly"; and two per cent did not answer
the question.

[2] For an analysis of some types of uncertainty that are
inherent in medical practice, as well as an account of how
medical students may learn to come to terms with such uncertainty, see Renée C. Fox, "Training for Uncertainty," in
Merton, Reader, and Kendall, op. cit., pp. 207-41.

both admitting uncertainty and being knowledgeable, it may be
presumed that they were motivated to seek and accept help when
they needed it as well as continually to acquire greater knowledge and skill. Advice from others clearly offered opportunities for such learning and assistance; yet, significantly, it
did not jeopardize the personal responsibility for patients
which physicians felt was essential to maintain. As one doctor
summed up this outlook:

> Having someone else's opinion may be very critical
> at times. There are so many nooks and crannies in
> medicine that unless you have the help of other
> people occasionally you're going to miss the boat....
> The important thing is to be aware of your limita-
> tions.

This is not to say, of course, that physicians always
defined advice from other physicians as a valuable learning experience, or that they were equally ready to accept help from
any physician who might be put in charge. As the following
chapter will indicate, whether or not they were even willing to
consider the merits of the advice given by a particular supervising physician depended to a great extent upon their assessment of his professional competence as well as upon his relative rank in the Medical College. Rather, what is suggested
here is that giving and taking advice was a general behavior
pattern among physicians which the norms and values of the
medical profession not only legitimated but, under certain
circumstances, required.

Administration

In contrast with patient care, the norms and values
associated with the sphere of activity which physicians called
"administration" permitted supervisory control through the use
of authority rather than influence alone. The three instances
described in outlining the authority pattern -- scheduling,
reporting patient contacts, and switching preceptors -- illus-
trate this relationship, for the decisions involved in each of
those instances were considered by the physicians to be essentially administrative in nature. About scheduling, for example,
a physician in the Clinic remarked: "Scheduling? That's just
administrative paperwork." According to one of the Residents,
filling out visit reports was simply "more paperwork," and concerning the decision to switch preceptors one preceptor noted,
"That's a policy matter -- you know, part of the administration
of the Program."

Observation of physicians in the General Medical Clinic
indicated that overt compliance with administrative decisions
was, in general, relatively predictable. But as might be expected, it was never completely so; deviations were also predictable, though they appeared to constitute a rather small
proportion of the total behavior observed.

Physicians in the Clinic, for example, did not invariably see all of the patients scheduled for them during a Clinic
session, or arrive exactly on time for their appointments in
accordance with the administrative request that they be prompt.

The reasons they gave for not complying were sometimes personal in nature, but more often they concerned an urgent professional obligation. "I'm late this morning because a patient of mine in the Hospital here just died and I had to talk with the relatives," explained a physician as he came hurriedly into the Clinic. Another, half an hour before the Clinic session officially ended, asked the physician in charge:

> Would you see my last revisit for me today? I just heard from one of my private patients -- sounds like she's in acute pulmonary edema and I think I'd better go see her right away.

Physicians in administrative positions expected and condoned such behavior, even though it was also a source of annoyance since it meant that work had to be reallocated. As one of the full-time staff members remarked,

> Sure it's hard on us when somebody doesn't show up. But if a doctor has to see a patient who's really sick, there's nothing we can do but accept it and divide his work somehow....After all, the patient does come first.

Apparently, following administrative regulations was not very important to physicians when the regulations conflicted with the professional task of taking care of patients whose need they evaluated as more pressing. Consequently they felt free to disregard administrative requests on occasions when such conflicts arose.

Administration vs. Professional Activities and Norms

That professional obligations took precedence over adhering to administrative decisions does not negate the fact that, in areas which physicians defined as "administrative," they were generally willing to grant those in charge the right to make decisions affecting their actions, a right which they did not concede in the realm of patient care. Examination of the prevailing conception of administration among physicians in the General Medical Clinic provides some explanation of this differential willingness.

By and large, physicians defined administrative activity more by exclusion than otherwise. That is to say, they tended to label as "administration" virtually any work in the Clinic -- and the Medical Center -- that did not involve caring directly for patients, teaching students, doing research, or the personal planning, studying, and writing entailed in these activities.

When pressed for a positive definition, some physicians who were informally interviewed specifically cited policy-making about organizational procedures, as in the case of the preceptor quoted earlier. But they were generally inclined to view administrative activity as, in the words of one of the full-time staff members, "paperwork and other housekeeping chores." An attending physician on the part-time staff explained the nature of administration in quite similar and deprecating terms:

> I've done administrative work and I don't particularly like it. That's just making out schedules and other paperwork.

Whether identified specifically as paperwork, housekeeping, or policy-making, however, physicians apparently agreed that administrative work was relatively non-professional in character, requiring little or no medical training for its execution and bearing only indirectly on strictly medical affairs.[1] This was implicit in the way they tended to contrast administration with taking care of patients and teaching, both of which manifestly did require medical training and were obviously medical activities. Thus one attending said,

> I'm glad I'm not doing any administrative work.
> I'd rather be seeing patients all the time...in
> my opinion, that's the doctor's real job.

Another reflected:

> Personally, I wouldn't enjoy being an adminis-
> trator....Administration is all right, I suppose,
> for doctors who aren't very good at taking care
> of patients.

And a full-time staff member commented:

> All the time I have to spend on administration
> doesn't leave me much opportunity to see patients
> or check students. I'd like to be doing more
> along those lines -- after all, that's what I'm
> trained for -- but I just can't find the time.

Such contrasts between administration on the one hand and patient care or teaching on the other not only suggest that administration was considered a non-professional activity; they also indicate something of the different attitudes and evaluations with which physicians approached the two types of work. They suggest that, as might be expected of professionally

---

[1] See Chapter V for an analysis of why, in spite of this view, there were pressures toward assigning physicians rather than laypersons to administrative positions.

trained persons, physicians generally preferred to be doing
professional work, which they valued highly, rather than administrative work which they clearly held in less esteem.

The prevalence of this outlook is indirectly corrobo-
rated by the answers physicians gave to a question contained in
the survey described earlier, which asked them to rank certain
activities "in terms of the amount of interest you have in
them."[1] More than half (63 per cent) of the physicians gave
first place to seeing patients, and roughly two-fifths assigned
this place to teaching or research (19 per cent and 17 per cent,
respectively). However, practically no one (one per cent)
rated administration as of primary interest, and approximately
four-fifths (79 per cent) of the physicians ranked administration last in terms of the amount of interest this activity held
for them.[2]

---

[1]Five activities were listed: "seeing patients in
private practice"; "seeing patients in clinics or wards";
teaching"; "research"; and "administration."

[2]More complete findings are presented in the following
table:

| Activity | Number and per cent of physicians who ranked activity first or last in terms of their INTEREST in it: | | | |
| | Ranked first | | Ranked last | |
	No.	%	No.	%
Seeing patients:				
in private practice	193	40)63	42	11)12
in wards or clinics	113	23)	5	1)
Teaching	94	19	--	--
Research	81	17	33	9
Administration	5	1	293	79
Total	486	100	373	100

The total numbers for the two ranks vary because some physicians did not answer part or all of the question.

These evaluations and conceptions of administration
help explain how physicians could find authority (rather than
influence alone) an acceptable type of control in the realm of
administrative activity. When physicians complied with administrative decisions, they gained freedom from a responsibility--
that of making the decisions -- which they considered more or
less onerous. Perhaps more significantly, since administrative
decisions covered only activities that they viewed as nonpro-
fessional or ancillary to their work, the norms of professional
practice were not called into question. This meant that physicians could comply with administrative requests without losing
their distinctively professional prerogatives; their individual
authority in the sphere of patient care remained intact and
their prestige as independent professionals was not threatened.

It should also be emphasized that in the CC&TP and in
the Medical Center generally, those who made administrative
decisions which directly concerned the work of physicians were
physicians themselves rather than lay persons. The norms and
values which led to and regulated the allocation of administrative work among physicians are described at length in chapter
V; here the fact of administration by physicians is noteworthy
mainly because it qualifies the analysis of authority presented.
That is, while the data in hand provide strong reason to
believe that a physician who holds an administrative position
can effectively exercise authority in administrative matters
with respect to other physicians, they provide no evidence

concerning what would happen if the administrator were a non-
physician.

Summary and Discussion

        The behavior of physicians in the CC&TP indicated that
they recognized and distinguished clearly between two normatively different types of supervisory prerogatives: the right
to make decisions governing their actions (authority), and the
right to give advice concerning their actions (influence).
They expected supervising physicians to exercise authority in
the realm of administrative activity; even though they might
critically review administrative decisions, whether or not they
personally approved of the decisions physicians were generally
prepared to abide by them. However, in the realm of professional activity -- notably patient care -- they expected to
make their own decisions, and the role of supervising physicians was confined to giving advice which physicians felt free
to accept or reject on the basis of their own independent judgment and knowledge. Underlying and legitimating the individual
authority (freedom of decision) which physicians claimed and
exercised with respect to patient care was a fundamental value
of the medical profession: personal responsibility for the
consequences of patient care given. At the same time, as professional persons physicians highly valued possession of medical knowledge and skill. Acceptance of this value conditioned
the exercise of individual authority by requiring that physicians be aware of their own limitations and therefore, that

they remain open to advice from other qualified physicians.
Simultaneously, it permitted supervising physicians to offer
advice and thereby fulfill their supervisory obligations. Thus
with regard to patient care, both the norm of individual
authority and of supervision through influence found formal
justification in certain firmly institutionalized values of the
medical profession. In contrast, administrative activity did
not call into play peculiarly professional values (except to
exclude them as applicable), undoubtedly because physicians
tended to view administration as a relatively non-professional
task which directly involved neither "medical" knowledge nor
"professional" decisions. Consequently, physicians were ordinarily able to comply with administrative requests without
feeling that their professional rights were threatened or that
they were shirking their responsibilities as doctors.

These findings resolve certain analytic problems even
while they raise others. First, they clarify what the planners
of the CC&TP took for granted when they instituted an official
hierarchy of supervision among professionals in the Program,
and they illuminate how it was possible for this hierarchy to
be not only maintained but accentuated over a five-year period.
That is to say, although hierarchical organization of professionals would appear to conflict with maintenance of the
individual authority which is functionally required for professional work, practice in the CC&TP indicated that it did not
do so. In large measure, the potential strain implied was

avoided through adherence to professional norms of behavior.
These norms did not require, as is sometimes thought, that each
physician be autonomous in every sphere of his activity, but
only that he be free to make his own decisions in professional
matters as opposed to administrative concerns. Nor, even in
the professional sphere, did the norms rule out the possibility
of supervision; so long as supervision came from a physician
and took the form of advice, it was within normatively acceptable bounds for physicians. Thus one of the institutionalized
mechanisms for reconciling hierarchical supervision of professional activity with maintenance of individual authority in
that sphere would appear to be the conception of supervision as
a formal advisory or consultative relationship, analogous to
the "staff-line" relationship found in business and industry.
(Another mechanism for avoiding strain, not so apparent in the
material presented thus far, involves the official position and
qualifications of the supervisor relative to those whom he
supervises; as will be indicated in detail in the following
chapter, physicians evaluated these carefully before seeking or
considering professional advice from a supervisor.)

Second, the findings suggest that supervisory relationships among physicians constitute a limiting case of the
general observation that the norms and values of subordinates
will affect, in greater or less degree, the extent and kinds of
control which those in superordinate positions may exert with
respect to subordinates. When physicians work in a formal

organization they do not come as disparate individuals with
vague, diverse, or radically conflicting expectations regarding
the nature of supervisory control they will properly exercise
or submit to, as the case may be. Rather, as has been shown,
they come as professionals, with norms and values regarding
supervisory control which are relatively well defined, shared,
and specific as to circumstance. Presumably, this is a consequence of the similarity and intensity of their prior professional education; during the course of their successive experiences as medical student, intern, and perhaps resident, they
have both the opportunity and the obligation to observe, learn,
and internalize professional standards for conduct in various
sorts of relationships with medical colleagues as well as with
patients and ancillary personnel.[1] At any rate, the fact that
physicians tend to share these standards _before_ affiliating
with a formal organization as fully-qualified doctors, and
regardless of whether they hold supervisory or non-supervisory
positions, is especially significant in the present connection.
For it suggests that in the case of physicians, of greatest
relevance in determining the extent and kind of supervisory
control that can be exercised feasibly are neither the norms of

---

[1] Theoretical analysis and empirical materials bearing
on the process of professional socialization are presented in
Merton, Reader, and Kendall, op. cit. See also the series of
"Working Papers in the Sociology of Medicine," sponsored by the
Bureau of Applied Social Research, Columbia University, especially Renée C. Fox, "A Sociological Calendar of Medical School
(1955-56, dittoed).

"superordinates" nor those of "subordinates" as such, but rather the norms and values of the medical profession at large.

When both supervisor and supervised are physicians, in other words, the control-oriented behavior of each is largely predetermined by established professional norms and values which both know and accept in advance. Relatively little mutual adjustment of role expectations is therefore required on the part of either person, and it is in this sense that supervisory relationships among physicians appear to constitute a limiting case of the principle cited.

Although this chapter could present no data concerning lay supervision, the findings imply that a great deal of adjustment may be required in supervisory relationships which involve non-physicians as well as physicians. If the non-physician is unfamiliar with professional norms and values, or unwilling to accept them as guides for his conduct with physicians, he may experience considerable frustration in attempting to exercise control, even in administrative matters. That such frustration actually is the lot of some hospital administrators who are not physicians has already been suggested by others[1]; but, although beyond the scope of this study, how common the predicament is and how it is resolved in practice remain important subjects for investigation.

---

[1] See, for example, Harvey Smith, op. cit.; Edith M. Lentz, "The American Voluntary Hospital," (Unpublished Ph.D. Dissertation, Cornell University, 1956).

CHAPTER IV

ADVISORY RELATIONSHIPS AND PROCESSES

When supervision of professional activity takes the form of an advisory relationship[1] it might be assumed that few professionals would object to being supervised. As the preceding chapter showed, they retain their individual authority to make professional decisions in such a situation and their professional values support the practice of consultation. However, supervision by means of advice is not the exact equivalent of consultation as this practice is institutionalized among professionals; although both involve giving professional advice, there are structural differences between the two

---

[1]It should be emphasized that in formal advisory relationships, the behavior required of the advisee by way of conformity with expectations is that he take the advisor's suggestions and opinions into account before coming to some independent conclusion or decision. Conformity does not require him to accept the advice in the sense of acting in accord with it; only when he ignores the offered advice in the sense of not even submitting it to critical review does he fail to live up to expectations.

This conception of conformity and nonconformity in formal advisory relationships is implied rather than stated explicitly in most analyses of such relations, no doubt because attention has been directed more to the question of whether and under what conditions advice is followed, than to the question of whether and under what conditions advice is critically reviewed. Yet it is the normative approval given to the latter behavior that in part distinguishes advisory relationships from authority relationships; see, e.g., Herbert Simon, op. cit., pp. 125-35; Harold L. Wilensky, op. cit., pp. 177-79.

relationships which provide grounds for expecting professionals
to reject supervision of their professional work unless certain
further conditions are met. Accordingly, the first section of
this chapter analyzes certain crucial differences between consultation and supervision. Later sections examine case materials and survey data in order to identify empirically some of
the conditions that facilitate or impede the acceptance of
supervision among physicians in an out-patient clinic.

Consultation Versus Supervision

   Section 8 of the recently revised (1957) "Principles of
Medical Ethics" issued by the American Medical Association en-
joins the physician to "seek consultation upon request; in
doubtful or difficult cases; or whenever it appears that the
quality of medical services may be enhanced thereby."

   There are, of course, many dimensions of the medical
consultation -- such as the degree of formality, the content of
the problem, and the amount of uncertainty involved -- that may
vary and whose influence on the nature of the relationship would
have to be assessed if a comprehensive analysis of consultation
were being undertaken.[1] Here, however, it is the general

---

[1]Such an analysis does not yet exist. However, for a
general discussion of consultation and other types of collaboration among professionals, see William J. Goode, Robert K.
Merton, and Mary Jean Huntington, op. cit., ch. 7, "The Scope
of Professional Activity and Interprofessional Relations." For
an analysis of the process of consultation between "outside experts" and non-professional members of an organization, see
Lyman Bryson, "Notes on a Theory of Advice," in Robert K.
Merton, et al., Reader in Bureaucracy (Glencoe, Ill.: The Free
Press, 1952), pp. 202-16.

structure of the relationship that is of interest.

Apart from its advisory nature, perhaps the most distinctive feature of the medical consultation is that it ordinarily exists as a social relationship only when physicians feel
personally aware of the need for advice and are therefore
actively motivated to obtain it. This felt need may stem from
a variety of circumstances: from a physician's own uncertainty
or doubt about a problem; from his desire to reassure a patient;
from his concern to avoid a potential malpractice suit; from
the express request of a patient or patient's relative for
"another opinion"; or from hospital rules which, in accord with
accepted medical practice, require consultation under certain
conditions.[1]

In all these situations, the physician customarily
"calls in a consultant" or "requests a consultation"; even
though he may offer the patient a choice among several consultants whom he considers appropriate, he is the person who

---

[1]The Joint Commission on Accreditation of Hospitals
(composed of the American College of Physicians, the American
College of Surgeons, the American Hospital Association, the
American Medical Association, and the Canadian Medical Association) recommends: "except in emergency, consultation with a
member of the consulting or of the active medical staff shall
be required in all major cases in which the patient is not a
good risk, or in which the diagnosis is obscure, and in all
first cesarean sections, sterilizations, curettages, or other
operations which may interrupt a known, suspected, or possible
pregnancy." "Principles for Establishing Bylaws, Rules, and
Regulations of the Medical Staff of a Hospital," prepared by
the Joint Commission on Accreditation of Hospitals, May 1955,
reprinted in Malcolm T. MacEachern, Hospital Organization and
Management (Rev. third ed., Chicago: Physicians Record Co.,
1957), pp. 211-23, at p. 212.

82

initiates the relationship with the consultant selected. In so
doing, he acknowledges his need for help from the consultant.
He also implicitly defines the consultant as a peer who is
worthy of his professional respect, and he establishes, usually
for a short time, an advisory relationship in which he volun-
tarily takes the role of advisee. He does not, however, obli-
gate himself to follow the advice he receives. Correlatively,
the consultant becomes an advisor only when he is asked for his
opinion and he agrees to give it; his role is confined to
giving advice _upon request_. The request itself implicitly enhances his professional self-respect, though it tends to be
seen as a particular honor only when it is made by a physician
whom the consultant himself respects as a professional peer in
the same field of medicine.

Because the consultation relationship among physicians
comes into being only on this voluntary basis and because respect for the consultant is thus an integral feature of his
status, there is reason to believe that few strains are gene-
rated for either party to the consultation.[1]

In contrast, the organizationally defined role of
supervising physicians in hospitals and medical schools frequently includes the obligation to give advice that is _unso-
licited_. In such situations the advisee presumably has the

---

[1]_Cf_. Peter M. Blau's analysis of informal consultation
practices among members of a government agency, in _The Dynamics
of Bureaucracy_, pp. 99-116, esp. pp. 103-09.

corresponding obligation to take this sort of advice under
critical review in the same way as advice which he had specifically sought out. But for both parties to the supervisory relationship, unsolicited advice has crucially different implications from requested advice.

Unsolicited supervisory advice -- however discreetly or
circumspectly presented -- tends to signify to the physician
who receives it that in some measure his competence as a professional is being questioned by another professional. He is
likely to react to this implied judgment of his competence with
some affect: to feel variously grateful, anxious, embarrassed,
offended, or angry,[1] depending on such conditions as the circumstances under which the advice is given, how much he respects the supervising physician, and how justified or worth-
while he believes the advice to be. The feeling-states, in
turn, serve as motivating forces toward subsequent acceptance
or rejection of the supervisory relationship. If for one
reason or another the advisee has sufficiently negative feel-
ings, his recourse may be to ignore further advice and thus
tacitly break off the supervisory relationship. As a last
resort he may of course leave the supervisory situation entirely by resigning.

---

[1]Cf. Lyman Bryson, loc. cit., p. 209, who indicates
that even in the case of the non-expert who has asked for advice, the expert's "mere existence is a mild slur on the competence of the men he is dealing with, and to whom he is giving
the supposed benefit of his superior knowledge."

It may be emphasized that rejection of supervision may engender tension between supervisor and supervised, but it cannot be formally penalized unless there is incontrovertible evidence that the rejection has resulted in malpractice of a serious nature; otherwise the whole concept of individual responsibility and authority in the realm of professional work would lose its meaning and significance.

The obligation to _give_ unsolicited advice is not without its potential problems for the supervising physician, of course. Like the consultant, part of the organizationally defined role of the supervising physician is to offer guidance to other physicians; unlike the consultant, however, he is sometimes required to do so without being asked. To carry out his role, he obviously needs qualifications that command the professional respect of those whom he supervises, as well as sufficient self-confidence to enable him to feel capable of offering adequate, informed opinions which he can be reasonably certain will not be rejected out of hand. As will be seen, if appropriate information on which to base advice is unavailable or if there is reason to believe the advice will be consistently ignored, the supervising physician is likely to feel frustrated and discouraged, sometimes to the point of being reluctant to continue carrying out his supervisory duties.

Thus once the possibility of unsolicited advice offered by someone assigned to give it is considered, for both advisor and advisee there appear to be some points of potential strain in the supervisory relationship. Whether actual strain and its potential consequence, rejection of supervision, will occur would seem to depend upon the existence of conditions which lead the advisee to respect the advisor and his opinions, and which allow the advisor himself to feel capable of offering adequate advice. Examination of certain phases of the history of chart review in the General Medical Clinic allows exploration of the significance and inter-relations of some of the more obvious types of conditions: rank, professional competence, and the availability of information.[1]

The Background of Chart Review

Chart review was briefly described in the preceding chapter. It will be recalled that this procedure required the

---

[1] Systematic, focused interviews with a large number of physicians concerning their personal experiences with consultation and supervision would undoubtedly serve to uncover additional relevant conditions, as well as to refine the general analysis of professional advisory relations presented above. In the setting of this study, however, such interviews were not feasible. To learn which conditions are associated with the absence of strain it is necessary to inquire about situations in which strain exists, and this is a delicate problem with ethical overtones in the case of advisory relations between physicians. Some exploratory interviews conducted by the investigator indicated that unless one is personally well known and trusted by the physician being interviewed, one is not likely to discover much more about strains in professional advisory relations than could be inferred from reading the official public statements of the American Medical Association. Information received from physicians who do know and trust the investigator is likely to be more enlightening, but it is also frequently accompanied by the statement, "This is off the record, you understand." Presumably as more physicians come to appreciate the potential value of systematic analysis of the medical subculture, the climate of opinion on these matters will change so that obtaining usable data will eventually constitute less of a problem for sociological investigators.

physician in charge to examine the recent notes made in the
charts of all patients scheduled for revisits during a clinic
session, to write out any suggestions he might have concerning
the care each patient was receiving, and to clip these suggestions to the charts for consideration by the physician or student with whom the patient had an appointment. An alternative
mode of making suggestions known was to write them directly in
the chart; eventually this practice was adopted in lieu of the
earlier, more cumbersome method.

Although physicians who served as instructors individually supervised the work of students who saw patients in the
Clinic, chart review was the only Clinic procedure designed to
provide overall, systematic surveillance of the work of both
physicians and students.[1]

Chart review was introduced during the year before the
CC&TP began full-scale functioning, as part of an attempt to
model procedures for maintaining standards of medical care in
the Clinic along lines current on the in-patient services of
the Hospital. On in-patient services, the Assistant Resident
in charge of a ward regularly reviews the work of the interns
who care for patients under his supervision. He examines
entries in the charts, checks the physical findings when he

[1]Conferences such as the History Meeting described in
the preceding chapter provided only limited and partial cover-
age, since the work surveyed was confined to that of the physicians on the full-time staff and to a selected sample of their
case load.

believes this is indicated, reviews the diagnosis, and in general closely follows the treatment and progress of patients on "his" floor. Since these practices were known to have salutary effects on standards of medical care provided in the ward setting, it seemed appropriate to those who were planning the CC&TP to try to apply the principle of systematic review -- though not the precise practices -- in the Clinic setting as well.

Accordingly, the Director of the Clinic (who was also Acting Director of the CC&TP and an Assistant Professor in the Medical College) began reviewing charts in the fall of 1951. He was assisted in this task by the CC&TP Resident, a young physician who was in his third year of postgraduate study of internal medicine and who held the rank of Instructor in the Medical College.

The approximately fifty attending physicians whose work was under review seemed to accept this sort of supervision with equanimity; although some inquired about the new procedure during the first few weeks, none registered protest. (If they had protested it could have been taken to mean that they were reluctant to have their work examined, an attitude that would be distinctly inappropriate in a teaching clinic.)

Together, the Director and the Resident regularly reviewed charts through the fall and winter. But in the spring of 1952 the Director needed more time to devote to other duties. Believing that the procedure was sufficiently well-accepted as an aspect of the routine of the Clinic so that he no longer needed to participate personally, he felt free to ask the Resident to continue reviewing the charts alone.

However, shortly after the Resident started to review the charts by himself, some of the physicians whose work was under review complained to the Director about the Resident and his qualifications for checking their work.

Complaints and Formal Rank

One attending physician, an Associate Professor of Clinical Medicine, said rather indignantly:

> What has he done that he should write notes to me? When I need advice from a resident I'll ask him.

Another attending physician who held the rank of Assistant Professor stated with assurance:

> That boy is good, but he's hardly dry behind the ears yet. I was taking care of patients before he even entered medical school, and I don't believe I need his help to continue doing it now.

Still another Assistant Professor told the Director:

> I think there are probably some things I could teach [the Resident] rather than the other way around. Frankly, I don't see the point in having him go over the charts.

Such comments, together with elaborations, were made by certain of the senior physicians in the Clinic, that is, men who held the rank of Assistant Professor or above in the Medical College. There were some eleven of these men serving part-time in the Clinic at that time; all were of course older and more experienced in the practice of medicine than the Resident. Four of

them complained to the Director, indicating more or less explicitly to him that they were prepared to ignore further advice from the Resident. However, none of the forty remaining
physicians who served part-time in the Clinic -- and who held
College appointments ranging from Assistant or Research Fellow
in Medicine to Instructor -- said anything to the Director that
could be construed as rejecting the Resident's review of charts.

That only senior physicians complained suggests that in
deciding whether or not they were willing to accept unsolicited
advice from the Resident, physicians in the Clinic took into
account the formal rank of the Resident and evaluated it relative to their own. Those who were on the lower rungs of the
academic ladder apparently saw nothing offensive in the suggestions he made to them about their work. (Or if they did, they
evidently did not feel that they were in a position to object
openly.) But some of the physicians with higher academic ranks
were obviously affronted, as their complaints indicate. To
them, the Resident was still a student, although in an advanced
stage of his specialty training, and they were easily reminded
of this fact by clear distinctions in dress: the Resident customarily wore the traditional House Staff garb of short white
coat and white trousers rather than the knee-length white coat
which other physicians wore over their street clothes while in
the Clinic. Undoubtedly senior physicians felt far removed
from the time when, as interns or assistant residents, they
looked up to residents on the house staff as valuable sources

of advice, information, and help in their work. That they did
not complain when the Director of the Clinic was reviewing
charts suggests that they were willing to accept unsolicited
advice from a physician whom they deemed their peer. But they
were not so willing to accept such advice from an obvious
junior.[1]

Complaints and Competence

Nevertheless, it would be premature as well as mislead-
ing to conclude that relative formal rank was the only condition which determined how physicians would evaluate a supervising physician. Examination of the content of the complaints
-- rather than the rank of the complainers -- suggests that
judgments and assumptions about the Resident's abilities as a
physician were also involved in their evaluations. Indeed,
while the complaints of course cannot be taken entirely at face
value, it should be noted that they contained invidious comparisons not between the rank of the complainer and that of the
Resident, but between the presumed bases of differential rank
in a medical school, namely differences in competence.

Quite apart from the Resident's day-to-day performance
in reviewing charts, which they could judge only from the brief
notes he occasionally wrote, physicians used various indicators
to arrive at an estimate of what might be called his general
competence.

[1]This interpretation is reinforced by examination of
the subsequent history of chart review, presented in a later
section of this chapter.

Among these indicators, the age of the Resident was not unimportant. Particularly for senior physicians, the youngest of whom was in his thirties, the manifest youthfulness of the Resident -- who was in his late twenties and who looked even younger than he was -- constituted strong presumptive evidence that he was less knowledgeable and skilled in the art and science of medicine than they. His relative youth also testified to less experience as a physician and therefore to a possible immaturity of professional judgment. As one senior physician put it, the Resident could not possibly have "the wisdom that comes with age and experience, the mature judgment that makes you a better doctor at fifty than you are at thirty."

There is indirect evidence to suggest that a reputation for remarkable achievements in medicine could, nevertheless, to some extent offset age as an indicator of professional competence.[1] As the survey data described in the preceding chapter showed, in judging the competence of their colleagues a high proportion of the physicians in the Medical Center placed great importance on having extensive knowledge of medical facts, and almost all of them attached great significance to skill in the realm of diagnosis. That they also considered other characteristics to be important when judging the competence of physicians in their specialty is demonstrated in Table 1. There a

---

[1] Cf. Paul F. Lazarsfeld and Wagner Thielens, Jr., The Academic Mind: Social Scientists in a Time of Crisis (in press), Chapter I.

TABLE 1

SOME BASES FOR JUDGING PROFESSIONAL COMPETENCE

Quality:	Physicians who Believe Quality is of "GREAT IMPORTANCE" in Judging Competence of Colleague (Total N = 507 for each Item)	
	Number	Per Cent
Skill in realm of diagnosis	477	94
Knowledge of therapy	462	91
Ability to establish rapport with patients	449	88
Skill in dealing with social and psychological problems of patients	401	79
Extensive knowledge of medical facts	357	70
Ability to work effectively with nurses and technicians	342	67
Ability to get along with other colleagues	284	56
Knowledge of community agencies of help in the care of patients	227	44
Ability to carry out research	87	17
Ability to put aside everything but medicine	65	13

number of qualities are ranked according to the proportion of
physicians surveyed who said the quality was of "great importance" as contrasted with "moderate," "minor," or "no importance."

Among the ten qualities listed in Table 1, the first
six stand out as items on which there was substantial agreement; two-thirds or more of the physicians attached great importance to skill in the realm of diagnosis, knowledge of therapy,
ability to establish rapport with patients, skill in dealing
with the social and psychological problems of patients, extensive knowledge of medical facts, and ability to work effectively with nurses and technicians.[1] Moreover, when asked to desig-
nate which one of the ten qualities they considered most important when judging the competence of physicians in their specialty, fully half (49 per cent) of the 483 physicians who answered
the question designated diagnostic skill as most important.

----

[1]Physicians were also asked, "Are there any qualities
not mentioned above [in the list of ten qualities] which you
consider of particular importance when judging students or physicians? What?"
Fifty-seven per cent of the 507 physicians cited no
additional qualities. The remaining 43% variously mentioned
qualities that could be categorized as follows: sympathy, kind-
ness, compassion (7%); dedication, motivation interest (5%);
intellectual honesty, integrity, ability to admit mistakes
(10%); intellectual curiosity, the critical mind (6%); other
intellectual and technical requirements for diagnosis and
therapy, e.g., ability to organize information (14%); emotional
maturity, self-knowledge, ability to work with others (6%);
being a well-rounded man, having extra-professional interests
(2%); all other and vague and unspecified qualities (5%). These
percentages add to more than 43% because some physicians mentioned more than one quality.

Four other qualities out of the ten accounted for most of the
choices of the remaining half of the group: 17 per cent viewed
extensive knowledge of medical facts as most important in
judging competence, 13 per cent emphasized knowledge of therapy,
11 per cent selected the ability to establish rapport with
patients, and 5 per cent emphasized skill in dealing with the
social and psychological problems of patients. (See Table A,
Appendix B.)

Further, which quality a physician thought most important had little relation to his status in the Medical Center.
With one exception, the quality emphasized did not vary a great
deal with the departmental affiliation, academic rank, or type
of appointment (full-time or part-time) of the physicians who
expressed opinions.

As Table 2 shows, the judgments of psychiatrists tended
to differ markedly from those of physicians who specialized in
medicine, surgery, obstetrics and gynecology, and pediatrics.
But the latter four groups, who constitute the bulk of the
clinical faculty, did not diverge widely from one another in
the qualities they were likely to emphasize as most important.
In each of the four departments, physicians emphasized diagnostic skill as a criterion of competence far more often than any
other single quality. Additional tables presented in Appendix
B indicate that among physicians of various academic ranks there
was even less divergence; those holding professorial ranks were
no more likely to focus on diagnostic skill than their

TABLE 2

JUDGMENTS OF MOST IMPORTANT QUALITY IN PROFESSIONAL COMPETENCE:
BY DEPARTMENT

	Per Cent who Believe Quality is "MOST IMPORTANT" in Judging Competence of Colleague				
Quality	Medi-cine	Sur-gery	Ob.-Gyn.	Pedi-atrics	Psy-chiatry
Skill in realm of diagnosis	58%	48%	44%	53%	8%
Extensive knowledge of medical facts	15	14	26	22	8
Knowledge of therapy	10	24	7	--	24
Ability to establish rapport with patients	10	6	14	15	30
Skill in dealing with social and psychological problems of patients	3	1	2	10	24
Other qualities	4	7	7	--	6
	100%	100%	100%	100%	100%
Total number	(188)	(135)	(43)	(51)	(37)

lower-ranking colleagues, although full professors and associate professors were slightly less likely to emphasize factual
knowledge than those in lower ranks. Moreover, there were
virtually no differences between the criteria used in judging
competence by full-time faculty members as compared with part-
time faculty members, and few differences between the criteria
emphasized by these two groups as compared with the group of
residents and research associates.

Taken together, these data suggest that among most physicians in the Medical Center, certain qualities were particularly likely to engender respect for a colleague's professional competence. Physicians in the General Medical Clinic apparently believed it improbable that a young man could have such qualities in any great measure. But if the improbable should happen and a young physician did demonstrate remarkable abilities, particularly as a diagnostician, his competence would presumably command their professional respect regardless of his age or rank. And because they respected his competence, physicians would be more inclined to consider his advice when he offered it.

However, physicians in the General Medical Clinic evidently did not believe that the Resident had such exceptional qualities. A physician who served part-time in the Clinic noted:

> In the final analysis, the diagnosis is the payoff. Word gets around here fast about people who are really terrific at diagnosing difficult cases.
>
> Actually, I haven't heard much about [the Resident's] diagnostic ability, which means that he's probably a good enough diagnostician but not what you'd call a brilliant one. If he weren't fairly good I don't think he'd have been kept on here as a resident after he finished his internship.

In this fashion physicians individually evaluated various facets of the Resident's professional competence. Those who concluded that they themselves were more competent than he found his review of their work offensive to their professional

self-respect; they could not respect him as a supervisor even
though they might respect him as a resident. Lacking respect
for him in the former role, they were not motivated to pay
attention to the unsolicited advice he offered. Although none
of these physicians formally resigned from the staff in protest,
in effect they broke off the advisory relationship.

Bases of Professional Respect

Thus far this account suggests that whether physicians
in an academic organization will accept or reject supervision
of their professional work -- and the unsolicited advice which
supervision entails -- to some extent depends on how much they
respect the individual who has been appointed as supervisor.
If the formal rank of the supervisor is approximately the same
or higher than their own, they are likely to respect him; correlatively, if they judge the professional competence of the
supervisor to be approximately the same or greater than their
own, they are likely to respect him also.

In principle, formal rank in an academic organization
is based on professional competence. This does not mean, however, that the two are so perfectly associated as to be indis-
tinguishable in terms of their consequences. Outstanding professional competence tends to command respect regardless of
rank, but high rank does not insure respect regardless of competence. It would seem that when physicians respect a colleague whose rank is higher than their own, they are paying
tribute not so much to his position as to his presumed or

demonstrated competence; available data, however, do not allow definitive conclusions on this problem.

Although these observations are drawn from a "negative" example, a case in which the person assigned to supervise did not meet the requirements of some of the physicians whose work he was supposed to review, as will be seen they are supported by more "positive" events, which occurred after the Resident was replaced as a reviewer of charts by another physician whose qualifications were somewhat different.

The Assistant Director as Supervisor

The complaints which the Acting Director of the CC&TP received about the Resident's qualifications for reviewing charts in the Clinic naturally distressed the Resident when he heard of them. Because he was leaving the Clinic soon to serve in the Armed Forces, however, he saw little point in trying to alleviate his distress through any definite action.

As might be expected, the complaints also troubled the Acting Director. He assessed the situation as distinctly un-desirable by remarking: "It's worse than if there were no supervision at all." Therefore he set out to improve the situation as best he could.

At approximately this time the Program began full-scale functioning, which among other things meant that the staff of physicians serving full-time in the General Medical Clinic was expanded to include an Assistant Director for Medicine. (The Acting Director was also officially named Director of the

Program at this time.)[1] It became possible for the Director,
therefore, to transfer responsibility for the review of charts
from the Resident to the Assistant Director. Like the Resident,
the Assistant Director was an Instructor in the Medical College;
unlike him, however, the Assistant Director had already
finished his period of resident study, and was somewhat older
and more experienced than the Resident though still less so
than the senior physicians. The Assistant Director had also
been assigned the post of Director of the Clinic; he was officially in charge of patient care and teaching there, a responsibility which the Resident had not formally held.

When the Assistant Director took over the duty of reviewing charts, so far as he knew he followed the same procedure as had the Resident during the previous few months.
Nevertheless, physicians appeared considerably more satisfied
with him than they had been with the Resident; none of them
complained about chart review to the Director after the Assistant Director was assigned to the task.

That the absence of complaints was not due solely to
apathy or to resigned acceptance of the seemingly inevitable is
strongly suggested by a remark which one of the senior physicians made to the Director:

> I think it was a good idea to bring in [the Assist-
> ant Director]. I knew him when he was at [another
> clinic] and there's no doubt about it, he's a
> capable man.

---

[1]For details about the composition of the full-time
staff, see Ch. II.

When physicians in the Clinic evaluated the Assistant Director's qualifications for reviewing their work, they found a man
whose formal Clinic status was higher than the Resident's and
whose professional competence appeared to be somewhat greater.
He was Director of the Clinic; he had a reputation for having
done "an excellent job" in his previous position as assistant
to the Chief of Service in another teaching hospital; he had
finished his advanced specialty training as an internist, and
the knee-length white coat he wore made it clear to attending
physicians that he was in the Clinic not as a member of the
House Staff but as one of them.

Even though there was still a gap between the Assistant
Director and some of the Clinic physicians in terms of rank in
the Medical College, judged competence, and age, it was less
than had existed in the case of the Resident. Considered in
conjunction with the Assistant Director's position as Director
of the Clinic, moreover, the gap evidently took on less significance. Physicians could more readily respect the combination
of qualifications presented by the Assistant Director. Accordingly, they could more easily accept the unsolicited advice
which he occasionally gave in the course of reviewing charts.
At the same time, knowing that he had the respect of his colleagues in the Clinic enhanced the Assistant Director's self-
respect and confidence, so that he was able to continue offering the advice with relative ease.

Advice as Conditioned by the Clinic Setting

In spite of having the respect of his colleagues, the Assistant Director did not always feel as confident about giving helpful advice as he would have liked. Noting that "In an outpatient clinic like this, about the only way you can keep tab on the care that patients are getting is to review the charts," he went on to say:

> Compared with bedside rounds, though, where you can see the patient yourself, reviewing charts leaves a lot to be desired. Every doctor knows that if you haven't seen the patient personally, you're vulnerable unless you make mostly routine suggestions. So that's essentially what you do in chart review.

This cautious outlook was not confined to the Assistant Director. At one time or another over the ensuing four years, similar views were voiced by the several physicians who succeeded him in the task. These physicians included the second Assistant Director, who served in this capacity from 1953 to 1954; the third Assistant Director, who served from 1954 to 1957; the physician who was co-Assistant Director for the 1956-57 period; and a few other members of the full-time staff who, after 1954, alternated with the Assistant Directors as "Officers of the Day" in the Clinic. The comment made by the man who was Assistant Director during 1954-57, for example, virtually echoes the statement of his 1952-53 predecessor:

> I'm not sure how much good this chart-checking actually does....When you look over the charts you can almost always find something to suggest -- a test that could help in the diagnosis, a consultation that might be useful, and so forth. But there's a limit to what you can say without seeing the patient yourself.

Such remarks serve to highlight another sort of condition which has consequences for both parties to an advisory relationship, but especially for the advisor. This condition has
little to do with either relative formal rank or relative overall competence, but instead is contextual in nature. Specifically, it involves the presence or absence of the patients
about whom advice is offered; more generally, it concerns the
availability of information upon which advice may be based.

On an in-patient service, those who review the professional work of other physicians have available not only the
charts of each patient, but the patient himself. The patient
is temporarily living in the hospital, and therefore the supervising physician on an in-patient service may conveniently base
whatever advice he offers both on what he sees in the written
record and on what he may choose to observe of the patient's
condition first-hand. The out-patient does not, of course,
live in the hospital but at home. He comes to the clinic,
receives medical attention, and leaves, not to be seen again
until his next appointment. He is not nearly so easily available as the in-patient to a supervising physician who wishes to
confirm an opinion or explore a hunch by examining the patient
himself. In special instances the supervising physician in an
out-patient clinic can, of course, make a point of being on
hand when a particular patient is due to come to the Clinic.
But he could not feasibly do this for every patient he might
want to see; to "catch" them all in a large, busy clinic would

be impossible.[1] Consequently he must rely more on written
records, which, as one physician noted, "practically _never_ tell
you everything you'd like to know, regardless of how complete
they are."

Regardless of how great the professional competence of
a supervising physician in an out-patient clinic may be, he is
thus sometimes in the unenviable position of knowing less about
the problems of a particular patient than does the physician
whose care of the patient he is supposed to supervise. Knowing
less and lacking a convenient way of learning more through
seeing the patient himself, the supervising physician tends to
experience uneasiness and anxiety if he attempts to offer more
than "routine" or fairly obvious suggestions. This tendency is
reinforced by his expectation -- based on generally accepted
professional norms -- that the physician whose work is under
review will justifiably take offense if he is offered something
less than informed, well-grounded advice. Consequently he is
likely to confine himself to suggesting the obvious. Even
though he might prefer to comment more incisively on various
aspects of the medical care reported in the charts, without
having seen the patients he is reluctant to do so.

---

[1] This is clearly recognized in the fact that large
teaching staffs are considered necessary for proper supervision
of undergraduate medical students who care for patients in an
out-patient clinic; if the instructor is to see each patient
whom the student sees, there need to be at least half as many
instructors as students, and a one-to-one ratio is believed to
be ideal.

It may be noted, however, that in spite of these con-
straints the procedure of chart review served certain positive
functions which appeared to justify its continuance. Occasionally what was "obvious" to the reviewer was not so obvious to
the physician who was taking care of the patient; consequently
the advice opened up new and sometimes desirable possibilities
for improving the medical care provided. Perhaps even more
importantly, the mere anticipation of review may be presumed to
have motivated at least some physicians to maintain high
standards.[1]

Summary and Discussion

Among physicians, supervision and consultation have
much in common. Both are formal advisory relationships which,
once entered, entail the obligation to give professional advice
on the part of the advisor, and the obligation critically to
review such advice on the part of the advisee. Supervision
differs from consultation, however, in that the supervising
physician must sometimes give advice that is unsolicited. Physicians tend to interpret unsolicited advice as an adverse reflection on their professional competence. Consequently if
they are to accept a relationship which involves this sort of
advice and still retain their professional self-respect, they
need to respect the source of the advice, the supervising physician. Whether they actually will respect him depends to some

---

[1] Cf. Peter M. Blau, The Dynamics of Bureaucracy, pp.
33-48.

extent on how they evaluate various facets of his reputed or demonstrated professional competence: his diagnostic skill, his knowledge of medical facts as well as of therapy, and to a lesser extent, his interpersonal skills in dealing with patients. In evaluating these qualities their point of reference is personal; if in their estimation the competence of the supervising physician approximately equals or exceeds their own, they are likely to respect him enough to accept advice from him. The respect accorded a supervising physician also depends to some extent on his formal rank, both in the medical school and in the immediate work context, whether ward or clinic. Unless a supervising physician of lower rank has remarkable professional accomplishments to his credit, physicians tend to respect him less than they do physicians whose formal rank is the same or higher than their own.

In turn, the role performance of the supervising physician is affected by the degree of respect accorded him; if he knows he is well thought of, it is easier for him to offer unsolicited advice. It is also easier for him to give such advice if he has the opportunity to see the patients whom his advice concerns. In an out-patient clinic these opportunities are rare (except in the case of physician-instructors who check the work of students) and so supervising physicians in that setting often feel constrained to confine their advice to relatively routine details of professional performance.

Clearly, these findings both extend and qualify those

reported in the preceding chapter. There it was suggested that
conceiving of supervision as a formal advisory relationship
serves to reconcile hierarchical organization of physicians
with maintenance of their individual professional authority.
This chapter suggests that to insure such a reconciliation,
certain other kinds of conditions are also necessary.

The formal advisory hierarchy becomes ineffective unless an additional requirement is met, namely, that the qualifications of the supervising physicians in the hierarchy be
such as to command the professional respect of those whose work
they review. Although physicians are not oblivious to formal
rank, professional competence appears to be outstanding among
the qualifications which they respect. In respecting and de-
manding competence physicians are not alone, of course, as
studies of men in other occupations and organizational settings
demonstrate.[1] That physicians are apparently able to enforce
their demand without difficulty, however, testifies to the
power of professional values in shaping organizational norms.

---

[1]See, e.g., Peter M. Blau, op. cit.; Alvin W. Gouldner,
op. cit.; Harold L. Wilensky, op. cit., Logan Wilson, op. cit.

CHAPTER V

ADMINISTRATION: A PROBLEM IN THE DIVISION OF LABOR

Like other professionals, physicians are trained to be experts in a particular field of knowledge and practice, and to place a high premium on the appropriate use of their specialized competence. In this respect, their values would appear to harmonize neatly with one of the major features of bureaucratic organization: the division of labor among organization members on the basis of differential technical competence.[1] Such an arrangement permits the various types of work in an organization to be done only by those who are properly qualified by objective standards, a principle which not only does no violence to professional beliefs but which associations of professionals actively endorse and enforce on behalf of their members. When applied to the case in hand, this principle would lead to the expectation that, just as bedside nursing was the recognized province of trained nurses and diagnosis of disease the province of licensed physicians, administrative activities would be the tasks primarily of experts or specialists in administration. In actual practice, however, as Chapter III suggested, certain

---

[1] A. M. Henderson and T. Parsons (tr.), Max Weber, The Theory of Social and Economic Organization, pp. 333-54.

administrative activities were not assigned to such specialists
but were instead made a part of the work expected of physicians
on the staff. And as Lewis and Maude have observed more generally, "the dilemma confronting almost every profession is
whether its members shall concentrate on 'strictly professional' work and lose their power to direct it, or learn administration so as to be able to remain in control of it, thus
losing the time to practise it."[1]

This chapter presents an analysis of how the general
commitment of physicians to division of labor according to
technical training is set aside with regard to administrative
activity. An understanding of the basis for this deviation
from "rational" organization is first provided through an in-
spection of the somewhat contradictory values and norms of the
profession, which constrain physicians to keep administrative
powers within the profession but at the same time, to hold such
activities in low esteem.[2] To observe that contradictory norms

---

[1] Roy Lewis and Angus Maude, Professional People in
England (Cambridge: Harvard University Press, 1953), p. 7.

[2] Sets of more or less contradictory norms and values
are not, of course, uncommon in the medical subculture; indeed,
they would seem to be more the rule than the exception. In
writing of these as embodied in medical education, for example,
Merton observes that "for each norm there tends to be at least
one coordinate norm, which is, if not inconsistent with the
other, at least sufficiently different as to make it difficult
for the student and the physician to live up to them both."
However, he goes on to say: "It is not that each pair of values,
or of a value and a practical exigency, are necessarily at odds;
they are only potentially so. The ability to blend these potential opposites into a stable pattern of professional

exist, of course, is to raise the problem of how and to what
extent the contradictions are resolved, both in terms of the
day-to-day behavior of physicians and in terms of the role expectations they hold. Thus the chapter proceeds to examine the
actual distribution of administrative work among physicians of
varying statuses in the CC&TP and in the Medical Center, as
well as to explore the institutionalized role expectations that
allowed physician-administrators to perform this required but
little esteemed activity without undue strain. Finally, the
chapter considers the potential significance which certain non-
institutional and non-professional factors may have in motivating some physicians to engage in administrative work.

Contradictory Norms and Values

As Chapter III indicated, physicians grouped a wide
range of activities under the rubric of administration, including routine organizational paperwork, "housekeeping" duties
of various sorts, and policy-making about organizational procedures. Some of the so-called administrative activities of
course had more technical medical content than others, as physicians clearly recognized if they were asked about specific
tasks. Nevertheless, when they spoke of administration generi-
cally, they tended to minimize the technical medical content

---

behavior must be learned and it seems from the data in hand
that this is one of the most difficult tasks confronting the
medical student." Robert K. Merton, "Some Preliminaries to a
Sociology of Medical Education," in Robert K. Merton, George G.
Reader, and Patricia L. Kendall, op. cit., p. 72 and p. 76.

and emphasize non-technical aspects, with the result that they ordinarily equated administrative activity with non-professional activity. Correlatively, they tended to deprecate administrative work and to consider it somewhat inappropriate for their time and attention, on the grounds that administration required no particular medical skill or knowledge, and consumed time which might be spent more usefully and valuably on tasks which did require medical training.

Underlying these assessments was their commitment to rendering service as a basic value and primary objective of the medical profession, and to teaching and research as closely related professional objectives.[1] While a non-medically trained person might broadly interpret "service" to include such administrative activities as policy-making or keeping records for a hospital or medical school, this was not the case among physicians; for them, rendering service meant caring directly and personally for patients, just as teaching meant instructing students on a face-to-face basis and research generally meant working in a laboratory.

---

[1] Section 1 of the "Principles of Medical Ethics" (American Medical Association, 1957) emphasizes service: "The principal objective of the medical profession is to render service to humanity with full respect for the dignity of man. Physicians should merit the confidence of patients entrusted to their care, rendering to each a full measure of service and devotion." Section 2 emphasizes teaching and research: "Physicians should strive continually to improve medical knowledge and skill, and should make available to their patients and colleagues the benefits of their professional attainments."

See also the Hippocratic Oath, which stresses service and teaching, but not research.

Commitment to these clearly professional objectives did not mean, however, that physicians were therefore in favor of assigning all administrative tasks to non-physicians as one might naively suppose. For they also believed that decisions which affected their work -- even peripherally -- should be made by physicians or, if delegated to others, should remain subject to the approval of physicians. Though rarely verbalized, the value-rationale for this norm was simple and straightforward: only physicians possess the necessary specialized and technical medical knowledge to take into account fully the potential implications which administrative decisions may have for the conduct of professional activities. At issue, in other words, was the positive value physicians placed on government of professionals by professionals.

Thus in the medical subculture, normative grounds existed which justified both assigning and not assigning administrative work to physicians, and which justified either acceptance or rejection of this type of work on the part of individual physicians. Militating against administrative work for physicians was the ideal of specialized service, teaching, and research as the primary activities appropriate for members of the medical profession; militating for administration by physicians was the ideal of professional self-government.

Distribution of Administrative Tasks among the Staff

However, whether or not a physician in the CC&TP engaged in administration was not solely or even primarily a

matter of his individual, personal preference regarding the
pursuit of one ideal or another. Rather, as this section will
suggest, assignment and acceptance of administrative duties was
closely related to the organizational statuses physicians held
in the CC&TP and in the Medical Center.

It will be recalled that formal responsibility for administration and professional supervision was assigned to physicians on the full-time staff of the CC&TP. In accordance
with tradition in the Clinic, certain of the administrative responsibilities were delegated to other specialized personnel:
administration in the realm of nursing was in the hands of the
Nursing Coordinator, and in the field of social work, in the
hands of the Social Service Coordinator. Overall administrative responsibility for teaching and patient care, however, remained an official role obligation of the Director of the Program and of the physicians on the full-time staff who assisted
him. At the same time, administrative responsibility was at a
minimum in the official role obligations of physicians on the
part-time clinic staff, whose major duties consisted of teaching and patient care.

As is well known, official responsibilities are not
always translated into behavioral reality. Yet observation of
the behavior of physicians on the full-time staff indicated
that they took their administrative role obligations seriously.
In fact as well as in principle, whether or not a physician in
the CC&TP engaged in administrative work was primarily a

function of his formal status in the Program. If he was a
full-time, salaried staff member, he was certain to be spending
some of his time on administration; if he was a part-time, unsalaried staff member, administration was much less likely to
take up his time. This was evidenced in a variety of easily
observable ways.

Along with representatives of nursing and social
service, full-time staff physicians regularly attended the
monthly CC&TP staff meetings, where the Director made general
announcements and the staff as a group discussed the Program's
policies, progress, and problems.[1] Physicians on the part-time
staff were invited to attend these meetings, but they virtually
never did so and the full-time staff did not in fact expect
them to be present. Indeed, the part-time staff of the General
Medical Clinic was never fully represented even at the special
meetings for attendings which the Director of the Program
called on an average of once a year in order to obtain their
opinions and advice on policy matters that directly concerned
them.[2] Moreover, there were other meetings held frequently and

---

[1]For a detailed description of these staff meetings as
they occurred during the Program's first year of operation see
Mary E. W. Goss, "Change in the Cornell Comprehensive Care and
Teaching Program," in Merton, Reader, and Kendall, op. cit.,
pp. 249-70, at 262-64. Intermittent observation of the meetings over the ensuing four years indicates that the attendance,
form, and content did not change appreciably from the description presented.

[2]Most of these men, as previously indicated, had private practices and therefore could spend only a limited,

regularly to accomplish more routine administrative work such
as selecting patients for family care and home care, or assigning grades to students, in which as a matter of course only the
full-time staff (physicians and other professional personnel)
participated.

In addition to participating as a group in meetings devoted to administration of the Program, physicians on the full-
time staff individually performed a variety of administrative
tasks. These included:

-- planning changes in Clinic routine and teaching
   emphases when these appeared desirable;

-- making routine arrangements for teaching conferences and lectures (e.g., seeing that a
   patient was present for demonstration; con-
   tacting men to give lectures and seeing that
   they were reminded of the date of the lecture);

-- making out schedules for students and attendings
   each semester;

-- answering written inquiries about the Program,
   as well as taking care of miscellaneous corre-
   spondence;

-- working out details of the CC&TP annual budget;

-- showing visiting medical educators around the
   Clinic;

-- writing annual reports on their activities in
   the Program;

---

scheduled amount of time in the Clinic. When meetings were
scheduled outside of that time -- as would inevitably be the
case for some since their time in the Clinic was staggered
throughout the week -- some attendings found it difficult or
impossible to arrange their other appointments so that they
could be present.

> — serving as physician in charge (later called
> officer of the day) of Clinic sessions, which
> involved daily scheduling, checking charts, re-
> viewing broken appointments, answering ques-
> tions put by nurses, students, and attendings.

Of all these tasks, only the last-named was shared by certain part-time staff members -- the senior physicians in the Clinic -- who upon request would serve as physician in charge of the session they attended each week. However, partly because there were not enough of these men available to cover every Clinic session and partly in the interests of consistent Clinic management, the bulk of even this type of work rested with the full-time staff.

What was true of the CC&TP with respect to the unequal division of administrative work between the full-time and the part-time professional staff appeared to be true also of the Medical Center as a whole. In the survey described earlier, physicians in the Medical Center were asked to rank several types of work -- "seeing patients in private practice," "seeing patients in clinics or wards," "teaching," "research," and "administration" -- "in terms of the amount of time you spend on them." As the first pair of columns in Table 3 show, full-time members of the clinical staff were somewhat _more_ likely than part-time members to report spending relatively much time on administration, and considerably _less_ likely to report spending relatively little or no time on this activity.[1] For

---

[1] The question did not specify whether physicians were to consider only the administrative activity they did in the

TABLE 3

AMOUNT OF TIME PHYSICIANS SPEND ON ADMINISTRATION AS RELATED TO TYPE OF APPOINTMENT AND ACADEMIC RANK

Relative Amount of Time Spent on Admin- istration:[b]	ALL PHY- SICIANS[a]		Full Prof.& Assoc.Prof.		Assistant Prof.		Instruc- tors	
	Full- Time	Part- Time	Full- Time	Part- Time	Full- Time	Part- Time	Full- Time	Part- Time
Much	35%	11%	48%	16%	33%	13%	28%	8%
Some	49	25	35	28	54	20	55	26
Little or None	16	64	17	56	13	67	17	66
	100%	100%	100%	100%	100%	100%	100%	100%
Total cases	(76)	(334)	(23)	(67)	(24)	(101)	(29)	(166)

[a] Excluding Research Associates and Residents who did not hold academic appointments, as well as those who did not answer the entire question. "Part-Time" includes physicians who are formally classified as "Geographic Full-Time"; these men are on the part-time staff but have their offices in the Medical Center.

[b] "Much" time designates rankings of 1st and 2nd; "some" time designates rankings of 3rd and 4th; "little or none" designates a ranking of 5th or no ranking at all.

example, less than one-fifth (16 per cent) of the full-time men

ranked administration as the activity in which they spent

Medical Center or whether they should also include work of this type that they did in other settings. Therefore it is likely that the rankings given by the part-time staff represent an over-estimate of the time they spent on administration in the Medical Center, since some might logically include the time they spent on administrative aspects of their private practice. In view of this possibility, the differences between the part-time staff and the full-time staff shown in Table 6 are even more remarkable.

comparatively little time, as contrasted with nearly two-thirds
(64 per cent) of the part-time staff who did so. And as the
remaining pairs of columns in Table 3 indicate, the differences
persist when the two groups are compared within each academic
rank. Among the full professors and associate professors, as
well as among the assistant professors and instructors, respectively, the full-time men consistently tended to spend relatively more time on administration than the part-time men.[1]

Table 3 also allows assessment of the relative influence of academic rank and type of appointment. Not surprising-
ly, it shows that within both the full-time and part-time
groups, high-ranking physicians were slightly more likely than
their lower-ranking colleagues to be engaging in administrative
work. On the full-time staff, 48 per cent of the full professors and associate professors reported devoting relatively much
time to administration, whereas the comparable proportions for
assistant professors and instructors were less: 33 per cent and
28 per cent, respectively. On the part-time staff, only 16 per
cent of the full professors and associate professors said they
gave much time to administration, but even fewer of the assistant professors and instructors did so (13 per cent and 8 per

[1]Although not reported in Table 3, research associates
and residents who did not hold academic appointments also
tended to spend relatively more time on administration than
their closest academic counterparts on the part-time staff, the
instructors. Among the 76 residents and research associates,
17 per cent spent much time on administration, 65 per cent
spent some time on this activity, and only 18 per cent spent
little or no time on administration.

cent respectively). Such differences are noteworthy, but they are relatively small in comparison with those obtained when full-time and part-time staff are contrasted, both as undifferentiated groups and within each academic rank. (See the rows of Table 3.) Thus in general, it would appear that while academic rank had some effect on the amount of time a physician in the Medical Center devoted to administrative work, the type of appointment he held was of even greater import in this regard.

The slight relationship between academic rank and administrative work observed in Table 3 was not contradicted in the CC&TP. Although physicians on the part-time staff participated less in administration than the full-time staff, those in the former group who did participate were likely to be the senior physicians, who held ranks of assistant professor or above. The proportion of those men who attended the special meetings for attendings called by the Director was ordinarily higher than that of their lower-ranking colleagues; the Director was more likely to consult them informally about administrative matters; and as has already been indicated, within the part-time staff only the senior attending physicians were requested to serve as physician in charge of Clinic sessions. Among physicians on the full-time staff of the CC&TP there were small, overlapping gradations in the proportions of time which men of different ranks estimated that they gave to administration. These estimates ranged from between one-fifth and one-third of the working time of residents to about one-half of the

working time of the Director, who was a full professor at the
time that he made the estimate.[1]

Professional Values and Organizational Roles: the
Part-Time Administrator

The qualitative and quantitative data presented clearly
indicate that administrative work was differentially distributed
among physicians of varying statuses in the CC&TP and in the
Medical Center. Considered apart from the fact that professionals were involved, this observation is commonplace if not
trivial; as is well known, the unequal division of administrative duties among members of formal organizations is the rule
rather than the exception in modern Western society. Viewed in
the light of the professional character of the membership,

---

[1] When the Director was an assistant professor, in 1952-
53, he estimated that he spent approximately one-third of his
time on administrative matters. Five years later, after he had
risen to the rank of full professor, his estimate was somewhat
higher: about one-half of each working day. The Assistant
Director for Medicine who served during 1953-54 and who held
the rank of instructor reported that he gave slightly less than
one-third (30 per cent) of his time to administration, while
his successor in the post during the 1954-56 period -- also an
instructor -- reported a somewhat higher proportion (40 per
cent). During 1956-57 the two physicians who shared this post
were each on a half-time basis; interestingly enough, their
combined estimate of the amount of time they devoted to administrative work amounted to 40 per cent also, but the physician
who was an assistant professor contributed more than half of
the total (25 per cent) while the man who was an instructor
contributed less (15 per cent).

Personal estimates of time spent on administration by
the remaining physicians who served in various years and positions on the full-time staff of the CC&TP are not available.
However, the Director reported that through the years, the
Assistant Directors for Pediatrics and for Home Care generally
spent between 30 and 40 per cent of their time on administration, as compared with a range of 20 to 35 per cent for the
Residents and Assistant Residents.

however, the observation is something more than commonplace.
For it suggests that the organizational structure itself served
as a mechanism for blending or reconciling the conflicting professional values described earlier: service and related professional ideals on the one hand, and the ideal of professional
self-government, on the other.

When administration is institutionalized as the responsibility of a minority of physicians, the majority are left
free to pursue professional service goals as well as secure in
the knowledge that their affairs are administered by fellow-
professionals rather than lay persons. Under this arrangement
the majority need experience no particular strain, in other
words, because their personal role obligations in the organization are likely to be strictly professional.

What is functional for the majority is not necessarily
so for the minority of course. Physicians who have administrative responsibilities are in a markedly different situation;
some degree of conflict between fulfillment of the two broad
ideals would seem to be inherent in their positions. But as
will become obvious, even for this group there is a built-in
structural mechanism for minimizing strain: role expectations
which combine administrative and professional duties, and which
therefore permit individual refusal or delegation of administrative work beyond a certain point.

The prototypes for the role of the minority who engaged
in administrative work -- largely the full-time staff -- were

the Chiefs of the Clinical Services in the Hospital. These
physicians held full-time appointments, and they were simultaneously professors and heads of their respective departments
in the Medical College (Medicine, Surgery, Pediatrics, Obstetrics and Gynecology, and Psychiatry). Their organizational
role obligations included both substantive professional responsibilities (patient care; teaching; research) as well as
administrative duties: representing the interests of their departments in the College and in the Hospital; appointing staff
members, assigning and coordinating their work; planning
changes in the organization or practices of their departments;
etc. That is, they were expected to be practitioners, teachers,
researchers, and administrators, and personally to divide their
working time in such a way as to live up to these several expectations.

This of course meant that the Chiefs could not possibly
be full-time administrators unless they shirked their more
strictly professional duties, nor could they spend full-time on
teaching, patient care, or research without neglecting their
administrative responsibilities.[1] Personal accounts of how
these men actually spent their working time are not available.
However, several physicians who had been in the Medical Center

---

[1] Contrast Chester I. Barnard, op. cit., pp. 215-16,
where the comparable "intermixture of functions" of the business executive is discussed as "a matter of convenience and
often of economy, because of the scarcity of abilities," rather
than as directed by professional norms and values.

for considerable lengths of time agreed that though there were
differences in emphasis from Chief to Chief, none of the Chiefs
focussed his time and attention on any one of his professional
roles or on his administrative role to the complete exclusion
of the others.

Modeled as they were on this multi-faceted pattern, the
institutionalized role obligations of other members of the
full-time staff also generally included professional as well as
administrative responsibilities. These are crudely mirrored in
the ways physicians on the full-time staff in the Medical
Center said they spent their time.

TABLE 4

AMOUNT OF TIME PHYSICIANS ON THE FULL-TIME STAFF[a] SPENT
ON FIVE ACTIVITIES

Relative Amount of Time:[b]	Seeing Patients in:		Teaching	Research	Administration
	Private Practice	Clinics & Wards			
Much	7%	57%	56%	47%	35%
Some	14	42	41	50	49
Little or None	79	1	3	3	16
	100%	100%	100%	100%	100%
Total cases	(77)	(77)	(77)	(77)	(76)

[a]Excluding research associates and residents who did
not hold academic appointments, as well as those physicians who
did not answer the entire question.

[b]See Note b, Table 3.

As Table 4 shows, the only professional activity which did not claim a substantial proportion of their time was seeing patients in private practice; as might be expected of physicians with full-time faculty appointments, 79 per cent spent relatively little or no time on this type of work. As might also be expected, however, the remaining professional activities -- seeing patients in clinics and wards, teaching, and research -- occupied some or much of the time of the vast majority, with only negligible proportions (1 per cent, 3 per cent, and 3 per cent, respectively) saying they spent relatively little or no time on such work. The amounts of time devoted to administration follow the same general pattern, although as compared with the professional activities, somewhat fewer physicians (35 per cent) reported giving relatively much time to administration, and somewhat more (16 per cent) reported relatively little or no time spent on this activity.

In short, no physician on the full-time staff was expected to spend all of his time on administration and apparently no physician did; the organizational norm was rather to combine administrative duties with professional medical duties, so that most members of the full-time staff were actually only "part-time administrators."

What this norm signified for physicians on the full-time staff, of course, was that their administrative obligations did not require them to reject the professional ideals they had been taught to pursue and respect. Indeed, being

positively enjoined by the organizational norm not only to
engage in administration but to care for patients, to teach,
and to do research as well, they had the right to delegate or
refuse additional administrative work when they could show that
such work encroached unduly on their professional obligations.
In direct or indirect ways they exercised these rights, as
brief examination of the process of balancing professional and
administrative work among physicians in the CC&TP will indicate.

The Balancing Process

In the CC&TP as in the Medical Center generally there
were no set rules regarding the proportion of time which full-
time staff members should devote to administrative matters.
And the outlook with which the Director of the Program approached the assignment of administrative duties was avowedly
flexible; he believed it was important for the full-time staff
to "spend as little time as possible on administration, but as
much as we have to so that the Program runs smoothly and
achieves its aims."

Nevertheless, it would seem that this flexible policy
of assignment operated only within certain generally understood
limits. As will be recalled, over a five-year period which
covered a number of replacements in staff, there was considerable stability in the proportions of time men in the various
positions gave to administration; the proportions ran from one-
fifth time to half-time, but never more.

Furthermore, how much time the Director and his staff

"had" to spend on administration was naturally related to the extent of the Program's commitments, and it is significant that these commitments were never deliberately extended or broadened before additional professional personnel could be appointed to take on the accompanying administrative (and professional) work.

For example, as early as the first semester in 1952-53 the Director and his staff recognized the desirability of expanding the very small home care service for patients which they had undertaken as part of their attempt to teach students the meaning of comprehensive care in various settings. Under the beginning arrangement, only a relatively small proportion of the students could take part in providing care for patients at home; because the experience demonstrably offered valuable learning opportunities for these students, however, it seemed clear to the staff that all students should be given the chance to participate, and therefore the number of home care patients should be increased. Also evident to them, however, was the fact that an increased number of home care patients would require more professional supervision (teaching) as well as more record-keeping, scheduling, and coordinative effort (administration) than anyone on the staff could take on without simultaneously giving up some aspect of his current duties. As was apparent from opinions expressed at a staff meeting where the problem was informally discussed, physicians could see themselves substituting home care teaching for one or another facet of their current professional duties, but they could not see

themselves substituting _administration_ of home care for any of
these duties.

The Director's decision to limit patients on home care
to a relatively small number followed almost automatically,
"because of limited personnel, and because all personnel involved [in home care] have...major responsibilities in other
activities of the CC&TP."[1] This decision was approved by the
CC&TP Advisory Committee, and not until a full year later
(1954), when additional funds made it possible to create and
fill the position of Assistant Director for Home Care, was a
systematic effort begun to increase the average number of patients on home care and to formalize associated administrative
procedures. To do so sooner would have been inconceivable to
the Director or to the Advisory Committee, all of whom recognized the right of staff physicians to refuse what appeared to
be an undue amount of administrative work, and who -- in this
case as in many others -- therefore did not seriously consider
making assignments which they believed would challenge that
right.

Thus to a considerable extent the process of balancing
professional and administrative obligations for full-time staff
physicians in the lower ranks took place when assignments of
work were made by those in charge rather than afterwards.
Acceptance by staff members of the combination of obligations

---

[1] As formulated in "Annual Report on Home Care Program
by the Resident, 1952-53," p. 1.

assigned to them was of course necessary to complete the
process, but securing this acceptance did not ordinarily constitute a problem, since the assignments consistently took professional values and norms into account and as a result tended
to include more professional obligations than administrative
ones. When, as in the case of Home Care, a potential organizational commitment threatened to upset that balance, it was the
organizational commitment that was at least temporarily foregone rather than the balance of any physician's obligations.

This is not to say that the content of each type of
obligation remained static for occupants of full-time positions
on the CC&TP staff. With the gradual expansion of the Program's commitments and the replacement and addition of a number
of staff members whose special interests varied, there was considerable shifting of specific duties among physicians, in the
professional realm as well as in administration. Whenever a
shift in specific administrative duties appeared desirable,
however, the Director customarily reallocated them in such a
way that for all physicians involved there remained sizable
proportions of time to spend on professional work.

In the course of assigning and reassigning administrative duties, the Director was quite aware that he was dele-
gating to others certain aspects of his own broad responsibility for administration:

> You can't operate a Program like this without
> delegating a good deal of the administrative work.
> I couldn't do it all myself even if I wanted to

> spend all my time on administration, which I
> certainly wouldn't like to do. So naturally I
> delegate some of the chores; there's no other
> choice if you want to remain a doctor, as the
> Professor [of Medicine] will tell you if you
> ask him.

Among the higher-ranking physicians who were responsible for
administration of a Service or Program, the right to delegate
some portion of the administrative work served as the counterpart of their staff's right to refuse an undue amount of administrative work; through delegation, the Director was able to
reserve some of his time for professional activities, just as
through the potentiality of refusal his staff did likewise.

Motivation for Administration

Although physicians on the full-time staff of the CC&TP
thus accepted administration as part of their work-load so long
as they were not expected to spend a high proportion of their
time on it, they also tended to express regret that it was
necessary for them to spend any time on this activity. In
casual conversation they consistently gave the impression that
they did not "really" want to be even part-time administrators,
and that they in fact engaged in administration only because,
as salaried full-time staff members, they were obligated to
do so.

> Though I enjoy being in the Comprehensive Care
> Program -- especially working with the students --
> I don't particularly relish the administrative
> side of the job. I do it of course, because it's
> necessary and it's part of what I'm being paid
> for, but I'd prefer to spend the time teaching
> and taking care of patients.

This fairly typical comment from one of the physicians on the full-time staff represents the kind of outlook physicians expect each other to have and to express. That is, if physicians did not openly view administration as a relatively unpleasant and professionally unrewarding task, they would be considered somewhat reprehensible deviants: doctors who had to a greater or less extent rejected the highest ideals of the medical profession.

However, so far as motivation to engage in administration is concerned, there is reason to believe that such statements tell only part of the story. Undoubtedly organizational requirements and economic incentives serve as factors which motivate physicians to accept administrative responsibility. But other factors may also be relevant; for example, individual career aspirations, interests, and experiences may play a part, as may the nature of the administrative responsibility itself. While a special investigation far beyond the scope of the present study would be necessary to determine the entire range and relative significance of such factors, the data in hand point to a few which may profitably be discussed.

Interest in Administration

When physicians in the Medical Center as a whole were queried privately and anonymously about the amount of interest they had in administration, their answers indicated that they were not completely united on this topic. In the entire group of 467[1] surveyed, nearly four-fifths (77 per cent) ranked administration as lowest in interest among the five activities compared, but 20 per cent ranked it in-between and three per cent ranked it high. Moreover, when these expressions of interest are examined in the light of the relative amount of time each physician said he spent on administration, it becomes clear that the two are related.

As Table 5 shows, among the three per cent who expressed much interest in administration virtually all reported spending relatively much time in that activity; among the 20 per cent who indicated some interest, fully 16 per cent said administration occupied some or much of their time; and among the remaining 77 per cent who had little or no interest in administration, 46 per cent or about three-fifths of the group did little or no administrative work. While the relationship is not perfect -- 29 per cent, for example, were essentially uninterested in administration but did much or some work of this type -- it would seem that in general, the greater the interest a physician had in administration, the greater the amount of time he was likely to spend on this activity.

The existence of this relationship tends to cast doubt on the assumption that physicians who engage in administration

---

[1]This number excludes those who did not answer the question. With the exclusion of research associates and residents who did not hold academic appointments, the total number becomes 394 but the percentages remain essentially the same as those reported above for 467 cases.

TABLE 5

AMOUNT OF INTEREST IN ADMINISTRATION AS RELATED TO AMOUNT OF
TIME PHYSICIANS SPENT ON ADMINISTRATION

Relative Amount of Interest[a]	Relative Amount of Time[b]				
	Much	Some	Little or None	Total	
Much	3%	--[c]	--[c]	3%	(13)
Some	6	12%	2%	20%	(95)
Little or None	6	23	48	77%	(359)
Total	15%	35%	50%	100%	(467)
Total Cases	(69)	(165)	(233)	(467)	

[a]"Much" interest designates a ranking of 1st or 2nd; "some" interest designates a ranking of 3rd or 4th; "little or none" designates a ranking of 5th or no ranking at all.

[b]See Note b, Table 3.

[c]N = 1, which is less than 1%.

invariably do so with reluctance, primarily because this type
of work represents a role obligation that cannot be avoided in
certain kinds of careers. For if role obligations alone were
relevant, then the degree of personal interest physicians expressed in administration would have been uniformly low regardless of the amount of time they were constrained to spend on
administrative work.

Even more to the point, comparison of the amount of
interest in administration expressed by two groups whose administrative obligations are known to differ in magnitude -- the

full-time and part-time staff -- would be expected to reveal no
marked differences if the assumption were valid. Yet Table 6
indicates that this is not the case. Although full-time staff
physicians were essentially no more likely than the part-time
staff to indicate that they had a relatively high amount of
interest in administration, they were clearly more likely than
part-time men to express at least some interest, and they were

TABLE 6

AMOUNT OF INTEREST IN ADMINISTRATION EXPRESSED BY PHYSICIANS
ON FULL-TIME AND PART-TIME STAFF[a]

Relative Amount of Interest in Administration[b]	Full-time	Part-time
Much	1%	4%
Some	41	15
Little or None	58	81
	100%	100%
Total Cases	(74)	(320)

[a]See Note a, Table 3.
[b]See Note a, Table 5.

less likely to express little or no interest. Further, these
differences persist when the two groups are compared within
each academic rank, as Table 7 shows. In every rank, propor-
tionately more of the full-time staff evinced interest in administration than did the part-time staff. Thus it seems

entirely possible that along with other incentives, intrinsic
interest in administration may play a part in motivating some
physicians to engage in such work.

TABLE 7

AMOUNT OF INTEREST IN ADMINISTRATION AS RELATED TO TYPE OF
APPOINTMENT AND ACADEMIC RANK OF PHYSICIANS

Relative Amount of Interest in Administration:[a]	Full Prof. & Assoc. Prof.		Assistant Prof.		Instructors		Residents and Research Associates
	Full-time	Part-time	Full-time	Part-time	Full-time	Part-time	
Much	--	2%	--	7%	3%	3%	--
Some	27%	15	56%	9	38	18	25%
Little or None	73	83	44	84	59	79	75
	100%	100%	100%	100%	100%	100%	100%
Total Cases	(22)	(66)	(23)	(98)	(29)	(156)	(75)

[a]See Note a, Table 5.

This crude hypothesis may be refined somewhat, since
Table 7 also shows that the nature of the connection between
physicians' interest in administration and their academic rank
varied noticeably with the type of appointment they held. As
might perhaps be expected of physicians whose primary commitment is to the private practice of medicine, a large majority
of the part-time men in every rank expressed little or no
interest in administration (83 per cent of the full professors

and associate professors; 84 per cent of the assistant professors; 79 per cent of the instructors). Within the full-time
staff, however, a distinctly different pattern prevailed. Some
73 per cent of the full professors and associate professors
said they had little or no interest in administration, but only
44 per cent of the assistant professors and 59 per cent of the
instructors held this view. Moreover, the views of residents
and research associates approximated those of the highest full-
time academic ranks rather than the lowest: 75 per cent of the
residents and research associates were not particularly interested in administration.

Stated in more positive terms, expressing some or much
interest in administration were one-fourth of the residents and
research associates, about two-fifths of the instructors, a
little over half of the assistant professors, and slightly more
than one-fourth of the full professors and associate professors
on the full-time staff. The trend that seems to be involved
here may be more apparent than real, since the percentages are
based on quite small numbers and the data are cross-sectional
rather than longitudinal.[1] Nevertheless, the absence of such a

-----

[1]Longitudinal data are generally obtained either through
retrospective questions or through a panel study which requires
respondents to answer the same questions at different points in
time so that change or stability in response can be determined
objectively. Without such data there is no certain way of
knowing, in the present instance, whether the expressed degree
of interest or promotion to the particular academic rank came
first. Thus one cannot tell, for example, whether the full
professors and associate professors described here had greater

trend for the part-time staff lends weight to the differences
among ranks in the full-time staff, and the overall picture is
sufficiently striking to warrant provisional discussion.

It may be that among physicians who are already more or
less committed to academic medicine as a full-time career,
interest in administration helps account for willingness to
carry out administrative duties only so long as these duties
remain within certain bounds. The relatively low amount of
interest expressed by those whose administrative responsibilities were likely to be greatest -- the full professors and
associate professors -- suggests that when administrative obligations become extensive, interest may be less significant
than duty in motivating continued fulfillment of those obligations. When such obligations are present but not so extensive,
however, as is likely to be the case for assistant professors
and instructors, the motivational role played by interest may
be more central.

Further, the fact that residents and research associates as a group expressed less interest than the full-time staff
but more than the part-time staff tends to emphasize the dynamic
significance that interest in administration may have for the
broad career decisions physicians make. Formally less committed

interest in administration when they were assistant professors
but developed diminished interest after they reached their current rank, or whether these men always had little interest in
administration, even when they were instructors and assistant
professors.

to a particular type of career than physicians who hold higher
positions on either the full-time or part-time staff, residents
and research associates must nevertheless eventually make a
choice. And it is plausible that their individual preference
or distaste for administrative work has some bearing on whether
they choose a career which they believe will involve much or
little of this type of activity. Presumably those who are uninterested in administration would be more likely to choose
private practice and less likely to choose academic medicine as
a career, while the reverse would be true of those who look on
administrative work with interest. This is not to say of
course that other, perhaps more important, factors do not enter
into career choices, or that residents and research associates
necessarily have realistic conceptions of the amount and kind
of administrative work they would ultimately have to face in
one or another type of career. It is to suggest, however, that
interest in administration may play a larger role in the career
choices of physicians than has customarily been recognized.

In this connection, various dynamic sequences of events
are conceivable. Possibly a slightly greater than average
interest in administration leads certain young physicians to
seek out work situations which require them to act as administrators at least part of the time. Some proportion of these
men may find the experience less interesting than they anticipated, however, and thereupon leave at the first opportunity
for a career which promises to involve less administration,

such as private practice. But another proportion may find as a
result of their administrative experience that their initial
interest was justified or even enhanced; all other things being
equal, such men would tend to focus on a career that involved
continuing administrative obligations. And it may well be that
certain of those who begin with no particular interest in administration but are placed in work situations which require
them to act as administrators part of the time (e.g., assistant
residents and residents), develop greater interest as a consequence of their experience, to the extent that they are motivated to change their career plans.

Whether or not these grossly oversimplified sequences
actually occur remains for future research to tell. To spell
them out, however, emphasizes the importance of examining the
nature of the administrative experience itself as a condition
which may serve to motivate physicians to avoid or select a
career which involves administrative work.

Types of Administration

Although this chapter has largely dealt with administration as if the activity were a single entity -- as indeed
physicians tend to speak of it -- analysis of such work in the
CC&TP reveals at least four types to which individual physicians
might be expected to react differently. Considering only the
types which emerge from combining extremes of content (relatively professional-relatively non-professional) and of level
(policy and planning-routine coordination), a crude though

empirically useful classification of administrative work is
evident:[1]

1. Policy-making and planning with relatively professional content:
       e.g., designing the CC&TP as an experiment
       in teaching and patient care.

2. Policy-making and planning with relatively non-
   professional content:
       e.g., allocating the CC&TP budget.

3. Routine coordination with relatively professional content:
       e.g., serving as Physician-in-Charge of a
       Clinic session.

4. Routine coordination with relatively non-professional content:
       e.g., scheduling doctors and students in
       the Clinic.

While virtually all physicians have had experience in both
types of routine coordination during the course of their in-
ternship or residency, the proportion who ever have the opportunity to engage in policy-making and planning is probably
quite small. Some of those who do have the opportunity, however, may find this sort of work considerably more appealing
than routine coordination, particularly if it involves content
that is relatively professional. For example, the physician
who was ultimately put in charge of Home Care in the CC&TP
noted:

> I didn't know at the time that I came [to the
> CC&TP] that I would be given as much responsi-
> bility in helping to shape the Home Care

[1] Cf. the discussion of "routine" and "critical" decisions in Philip Selznick, Leadership in Administration
(Evanston, Ill.: Row, Peterson and Co., 1957), pp. 29-64.

>Program....The fact that I have that responsi-
>bility has been very gratifying to me, and a
>great source of stimulation; in this setting
>there is a good opportunity to satisfy a
>certain creative urge.

Others may simply have their original views confirmed, as was

the case with one of the Assistant Directors in the CC&TP:

>After this year I'm going into private practice.
>For my taste, this job involves more organizing
>and planning and coordination than I'm inter-
>ested in doing for any length of time.

The chance to try their hands at being what one sociologist[1]

has called "program professionals" rather than simply "techni-

cian professionals" may, in other words, reveal new and attrac-

tive vistas of work for certain physicians but not for others.

The problem of how and to what extent such differential

reactions occur is as yet too complex and unexplored to be dis-

cussed here. It should be noted, however, that the physician

who learns that he enjoys policy-making and planning and who

enters a work situation which permits this activity ordinarily

does not simultaneously reject more strictly professional ac-

tivities. Rather, being motivated to do both, as described

earlier he attempts to balance them. This is characteristic

of the "program professional," who

>combines his high professional identification and
>his desire for full utilization of his profes-
>sional skills with an interest in heavy program
>impact within his area of specialization....This
>Program Professional's concern with the direction
>of policy within his area does not violate [pro-
>fessional] norms...he shares the technician

---

[1]Harold L. Wilensky, op. cit., pp. 129-44.

Professional's desire to render competent, efficient professional services, which occasions
some difficulty. The role orientation of this
type involves a constant balancing off of commitment to program vs. commitment to quality
work....[1]

Summary and Discussion

The medical profession is committed to a pair of values
which have somewhat contradictory implications for the allocation of administrative work. The ideal of specialized service,
teaching, and research as the only appropriate activities for
members of the profession militates against administrative work
for physicians, whereas the value placed on government of professionals by professionals favors it.

As might be anticipated in the case of such basic professional values, both were reflected to some extent in the
specific role expectations, norms, and behavior of physicians
in the CC&TP and in the Medical Center. The values did not
remain openly contradictory, however; in some measure the
organizational structure served to reconcile and blend them, so
that there was less strain for physicians than might otherwise
have been the case. A major mechanism in this respect was the
division of the professional staff into two groups with overlapping but somewhat different sets of role obligations in the
organization. One large group -- the unsalaried, part-time
staff -- served primarily as teachers and practitioners. The
other small group, composed of salaried, full-time staff members,

---

[1] Wilensky, op. cit., p. 133 and p. 141.

generally served not only as teachers and practitioners, but as researchers and administrators as well. In effect, this arrangement virtually eliminated the problem of choosing between the two values for the majority of physicians, who as part-time men could go about their professional work without much concern regarding administration, since they knew it was in the hands of fellow-professionals. The arrangement, of course, affected the minority charged with administrative duties somewhat differently. Because of the dual nature of their role obligation (professional and administrative), full-time men did not have to choose in any absolute sense between adherence to one or the other value. However, they did face the problem of balancing the two types of obligations in terms of time. In this respect they were aided by informal norms prevailing among the full-time staff. It was generally under-stood that there were certain proportions of time -- which varied somewhat according to rank -- within which assignments of administrative work would be made and accepted, and beyond which potential assignments could be rejected or delegated in favor of professional work. The strength of these norms was such that if a potential organizational commitment threatened to disturb the agreed-upon balance, it was the organizational commitment that was at least temporarily foregone rather than the balance. Thus the process of balancing professional and administrative obligations entailed fewer problems for the full-time staff than might be supposed; the process was less a

matter of personal adjustment and decision on the part of each
physician than an institutionalized, professionally-approved
procedure for assigning and accepting work.

Although physicians who do administrative work customarily deplore the fact that they "have" to spend time on this
activity as part of their job, the data suggest that at least
some of these physicians actually enjoy such work, particularly
when it involves policy-making and planning in relatively professional areas, and so long as they are not committed to it on
a full-time basis. More generally, there is some indication
that the factors which motivate physicians to engage in administration include not only economic incentives and perceived
organizational requirements, but positive interest in certain
types of administration as well. Further research on the range
and relative significance of such motivating factors is clearly
necessary.

In conclusion, it should be noted that where professional norms and bureaucratic principles diverged, the allocation of administrative work among physicians tended to follow
the former rather than the latter. Physicians who engaged in
administration were not formally trained as administrators and
they were not expected to view this activity as their major
duty, as they might have been if such work had been assigned
bureaucratically, on the basis of specialized competence in
administration. Nevertheless, it seems fairly clear that the
relatively non-bureaucratic arrangement which prevailed was

more functional for individual physicians than if there had been "expert administrators" who were not professionals in charge. Which arrangement is more functional for achieving organizational aims, however, remains for future research to tell. This account can only serve to suggest that the aims of the organization under review did not appear to be hampered by the relatively non-bureaucratic method of dividing administrative tasks that has been described.

CHAPTER VI

CONCLUSION

The broad purpose of this case study of physicians was
to explore the nature of professional roles and relationships
as they are structured in a complex formal organization. More
particularly, information was sought which would help clarify
certain problems in the sociology of the professions that stem
from the apparent incompatibility of bureaucratic organization
and professional work, norms, and values. The information collected has been presented and analyzed in preceding chapters.
It remains, therefore, to review the findings within a broader
perspective and to consolidate what has been learned in the
form of provisional hypotheses for future systematic research.

The Impact of Professional Values on Work Roles

On the basis of his examination of the roles assigned
to and played by staff experts in several labor unions,
Wilensky[1] found that these staff roles were shaped not so much
by the experts themselves as by the non-professional line
officials of the unions, within whose power it was to set work
objectives for the experts, and sometimes to specify work procedures as well. In the words of the subtitle Wilensky chose

---

[1] Harold L. Wilensky, op. cit.

to give his report, there were decided "organizational pressures on professional roles." In a similar vein, Merton's
analysis[1] of the role of the intellectual in public bureaucracy stresses the significance of the organizational forces
which impinge upon experts in social science and law who are
employed by the government. More specifically, "...the state
bureaucracy exerts a pressure upon the alienated intellectual
to accommodate himself to the policies of those who make the
strategic decisions, with the result that, in time, the role of
the one-time alienated intellectual may become indistinguish-
able from that of the technician."[2]

With particular reference to physicians who work in
bureaucratic settings, both Field[3] and Ben-David[4] present evidence which suggests that under certain circumstances, organizational pressures also play an important part in molding the
roles of these professionals. Studying a group of physicians
employed by the Sick Fund of the General Federation of Labor in
Israel, Ben-David found that "the transfer of responsibility
from the individual doctor to the institution was apparently
perceived by the doctors as a loss of status,"[5] which in turn

---

[1]Robert K. Merton, "Role of the Intellectual in Public
Bureaucracy," loc. cit., pp. 207-24.

[2]Ibid., p. 214.

[3]Mark G. Field, op. cit.

[4]Joseph Ben-David, op. cit.

[5]Ibid., p. 10.

led to apathy with respect to the professional role or, alternatively though less frequently, to an inappropriately great
emphasis on either the "service" or "science" components of the
professional role in an effort to achieve higher status.[1]   In
Soviet Russia, as Field notes, the medical profession is currently trained by and under the direct control of the government. In deciding who is sick and who is well, who needs medical treatment and who does not, Soviet physicians must take
into account the stated needs of the government for manpower.
To the extent that these physicians make such decisions according to governmental dictum rather than their own professional
judgment they are, of course, relinquishing their professional
role obligation to render unbiased service to patients.

In contrast with the foregoing analyses, the subtitle
of the present study calls attention to "professional pressures
on organizational roles." .For a major conclusion of this study
is that in the type of situation here examined, the professional norms and values of physicians set distinct limits on
how organizational needs for policy-making, coordination, and
supervision will be met, and thus markedly affect definition of
the organizational roles of the physicians involved. Organizational pressures exist, of course, but their impact is regularly tempered by built-in professional counter-pressures, to the
extent that the latter appear highly significant in accounting

---

[1]Ibid., pp. 30-31.

for the nature of physicians' organizational roles.

Evidence for the impact of professional norms is largely qualitative and indirect. Indeed, what is here advanced as
a conclusion may best be seen as a provisional hypothesis which
clearly requires more systematic and extensive investigation in
similar contexts than was possible in this exploratory study.
Yet within the limits of available data the findings are consistent.

As has been shown, in two significant areas -- authority relationships and the division of labor -- the organizational roles of physicians were somewhat contrary to what might
have been expected if purely bureaucratic standards had been
operative, and much more in accord with what would be anticipated had professional norms and values guided the definition
of roles. Further support for the hypothesis is furnished by
certain sequences of events that occurred in the CC&TP. When,
in the case of chart review, some physicians complained about a
supervising physician who did not meet their professional
standards of training and competence, their complaints were
heeded and the physician was replaced by one whose qualifications were higher. And in the case of the Home Care Program,
physicians effectively resisted expansion -- even though expansion represented a logical and desirable fulfillment of an
organizational commitment -- until it could be accomplished
without violating their professional norms concerning the
amount of time a physician might reasonably spend on

administration as compared with more clearly professional activities. Finally and perhaps most importantly, it was physicians themselves who were responsible for instituting the CC&TP, and who designed their own organizational roles in accordance with prevailing professional norms. The fact that in doing so they did not meet with opposition from non-physicians in the Medical Center is easy to overlook, yet it represents strong evidence in favor of the hypothesis advanced.

Organizational Pressures

To emphasize both the existence and the effectiveness of professional pressures on organizational roles in the case examined thus appears reasonably well justified. However, to infer from this emphasis that physicians were entirely free from organizational pressures in shaping their roles would be incorrect. Such pressures existed and they too were effective. But because they were formulated primarily within the framework of professional values rather than bureaucratic standards, they were not conspicuous and they appeared to pose no particular threat to the physicians involved. The pressures, in other words, were organizational but they were not rigidly bureaucratic; organizational needs for policy-making, supervision and coordination were met, but not according to a strict bureaucratic pattern.

More particularly, where there might have been conflict between bureaucratic standards and the professional values of physicians, in the CC&TP and in the Medical Center generally

there were instead institutionalized structural mechanisms
which served to reconcile potentially discordant elements in
ways that were approved by physicians as well as functional for
their work. As a brief review of the mechanisms uncovered in
this study will show, they also served to give the organization
a distinctive character, a character of a type that Weber did
not explicitly describe, but which perhaps most closely ap-
proximates what Logan Wilson has called "semi-bureaucracy."
(As will also be suggested, this type appears to combine what
Gouldner has identified as the "representative" pattern of
bureaucracy as well as what a later section in this chapter
will identify as "advisory bureaucracy.")

Potential Strains and Mechanisms for their Resolution

As is commonly believed and as this study found to be
the case, physicians place high value on assuming personal responsibility and exercising individual authority in making professional decisions; accordingly, their role expectations
emphasize independence in the realm of professional work. The
hierarchical authority structure characteristic of bureaucratic
organization as delineated by Weber clearly conflicts with such
role expectations, since there, in the interest of the organization as a whole, decisions are commonly subject to direction, review, and possible revision by those who hold superordinate positions in the hierarchy.

To find that physicians in the CC&TP held positions
that were hierarchically organized seemed, therefore, to

constitute evidence for the existence of bureaucracy and consequently, for the anticipation that there would be continuing
conflict or strain as a result of curtailed individual authority. Yet conflict was not apparent, and closer examination of
role relationships between those who were formally superordinate provided a provisional explanation.

Individual authority in making professional decisions
was not curtailed, by virtue of the fact that the hierarchy of
positions entailed two different types of control relationships
which varied according to the area of work (professional or administrative) considered. Only in the realm of administration
did the supervisory hierarchy refer to a set of formal authority relationships, i.e., to the right to make decisions with
which subordinates have an obligation to comply. In the realm
of professional work, the hierarchy referred to formal role relationships that are most properly termed advisory, i.e., the
right to give advice which subordinates are obliged to take
under critical review, but not necessarily to follow in making
their decisions. It may be emphasized that this was not merely
a matter of differences in the phrasing of requests in the two
areas, but of differences in expectations regarding compliance
as well.

Thus with respect to the organization of authority
among physicians, a major mechanism for reconciling bureaucratic standards with professional values would seem to be a
dual control system within a single hierarchy of positions.

Structured authority relationships in the area of administration make coordination of effort possible and relatively predictable; structured advisory relationships in the realm of professional work allow systematic supervision and yet leave intact each physician's individual authority.[1] A single hierarchy which encompasses both kinds of control relationships not only tends to insure maintenance of professional norms and values; it also serves to reduce the likelihood of formulating conflicting policies in the two areas of work.

However, it would further seem that these control relationships cannot be effectively maintained except under certain conditions which, subject to more extensive investigation, may therefore be viewed as subsidiary mechanisms for reconciling bureaucratic standards with professional values in the realm of control.

Among these conditions, the data suggest that where professional supervision -- i.e., the formal advisory relationship -- is concerned, the qualifications of those who are assigned to supervise must be taken into account, as must the supervisor's opportunity to obtain information on which to base advice.

---

[1]Formal advisory relationships do not, of course, permit the same degree of predictability as formal authority relationships; the former introduce an element of uncertainty that is largely absent in an effective authority relationship. However, as a later section will suggest, such relative uncertainty and unpredictability may not be as dysfunctional for the achievement of organizational aims as has sometimes been suggested.

Even though the supervisor offers only advice rather than orders, in the nature of the supervisory situation (and in contrast with the consultation situation where advice is given only upon request) the supervisor's advice is often unsolicited. Regardless of the qualifications of the supervisor, physicians are liable to interpret unsolicited advice as an adverse reflection on their professional competence. Nevertheless, because they are trained to value competence and at the same time to believe that no physician is so proficient as to be right all of the time or equally informed about every area of medicine, they are likely to experience supervisory advice as helpful and to review it carefully if they respect the supervisor as their professional peer or superior.

In the medical subculture, this means that the supervisor must first of all be a physician. But in addition to this basic qualification, commanding the respect necessary for unsolicited advice to be critically reviewed (though not necessarily followed) requires that the supervising physician be known to be at least as competent, if not more competent, in the science and art of medicine than those whom he supervises. Judging the competence of physicians is not a cut-and-dried, easily codified procedure, even when it is done by fellow-physicians trained in the same medical specialty. Yet as informal interviews and survey data suggested, there are certain attributes which most physicians consider important and which they regularly seem to take into account in judging the professional competence of a colleague: diagnostic skill, knowledge of medical facts as well as of therapy, and to a lesser extent, interpersonal skills in dealing with patients.

Commanding respect as a supervisor of professional work would also seem to depend somewhat on the formal rank of the supervisor in the organization; when this is as high or higher than the ranks held by the physicians who are supervised, respect is more likely. Although this study could provide no definitive evidence as to the relative significance of formal rank versus professional competence as bases for respect, it appears that in the eyes of physicians, rank may well be less important than demonstrated professional competence. Finally, and quite apart from these two kinds of qualifications, the supervisor must have appropriate information which is specific to the case at hand; if he has not had the opportunity to examine personally the patient whom his advice concerns, he is in danger of losing respect unless the advice is confined to relatively routine aspects of patient care.

Because, in the situation studied, the same physicians who served as supervisors of professional work also served as administrative officers, it was impossible to examine independently what supervisory qualifications might be necessary in order for effective control relationships to exist in the realm of administration as contrasted with professional work. However, there was some indication that formal rank is considerably more important in the administrative context than in the context

of professional activity, provided the rank is held by a
physician.

Although physicians consider administration to be a
non-professional activity which requires no particular training
or skill, they nevertheless recognize that seemingly administrative decisions may sometimes have close bearing on their
professional work; accordingly, there is pressure toward filling administrative positions with men who can be counted on to
know, understand, and abide by professional norms and values in
formulating and carrying out organizational policy. It may be
that all such men need not be physicians; if they are physicians, however, it would seem that they stand a greater chance
of maintaining effective authority relationships with the professionals under their charge, since they tend to know "automatically" what administrators who are non-physicians must
sometimes learn laboriously: the probable limits of their
authority in administrative matters. It is not, in other
words, so much the extent of the physician-administrator's professional competence that secures compliance with his administrative decisions as it is his intimate and first-hand knowledge of the medical subculture, which usually enables him to
know in advance what decisions he may make with assurance that
they will be accepted. More research is patently needed on
this problem of course; however it may be provisionally suggested that the more closely the content of an administrative
decision approaches the realm of professional work and the less

routine it is, the greater is the demand that the decision be made by a physician-administrator rather than by a non-physician of the same rank. Whether a physician or a non-physician did the daily scheduling in the General Medical Clinic, for example, did not appear to be of great moment to the doctors there; however, it was important to them that physicians be the persons who planned the CC&TP.

The demand for physicians as administrators conflicts, of course, with the bureaucratic norm of dividing organizational work on the basis of specialized competence; although the physician is trained to be a specialist in medical knowledge and practice, only rarely is he a trained specialist in administration. More significantly, however, the demand also conflicts with a professional norm, in that to engage in administrative work represents a departure from the professional ideal of patient-care, teaching, and research as the major types of work appropriate for a doctor. Consequently, physicians tend to view administration as a less prestigeful kind of work and are not, by and large highly motivated to be administrators. Nevertheless, it would seem that some proportion must be administrators if effective authority relationships are to be maintained, and if the value physicians place on professional self-government is to be upheld.

They need not, however, be _full-time_ administrators, and in this observation lies the key to the organizational mechanism which at least partly resolves the problem:

institutionalization of administration as a part-time occupational role for a minority of the physicians who work on the
staff, a minority who hold salaried, full-time positions.
Through this arrangement, the majority of the physicians in the
organization are left free to pursue more strictly professional
work objectives, and the minority who do engage in administration are not thereby forced to abandon the professional work
for which they were specifically trained. The latter group
may, of course, face the problem of balancing their professional ahd administrative role obligations in terms of time, but
because there exist among physicians informal norms concerning
the proportions of time that are appropriate to devote to each
type of obligation, the existence of tensions in this respect
tends to be minimized though clearly the tensions are not
entirely eliminated. Further, the fact that they are salaried,
full-time staff members enhances the probability that they will
be motivated to live up to their administrative role obligations, although clearly other motivating forces must also be
explored and taken into account.

This analysis of structural mechanisms for reconciling
bureaucratic standards with professional values and norms is
obviously far from complete, based as it is on examination of
selected aspects of only two areas of potential strain --
authority and the division of labor -- in one particular organization. Yet these areas are vital in characterizing and
differentiating various types of formal organization, and thus

the analysis draws attention to the problem of how to classify,
in meaningful sociological terms, the kind of staff organization observed: a kind in which physicians apparently are not
only able but willing to work without experiencing noticeable
strain. The analysis also raises the problem of why this kind
of staff organization does not always occur among physicians,
and, more generally, among professionals in other fields who
work in an organized context. These problems are considered
below in sequence, and followed by brief discussion of some
additional directions for further sociological research.

The Problem of Classification

Clearly, the staff organization described is neither a
"pure" case of bureaucracy or of a "company of equals." As has
been suggested, professional pressures prevent the former while
organizational pressures prevent the latter. Rather, closely
interwoven in the organization are both bureaucratic and egalitarian elements: hierarchical authority roles in the administrative sphere exist along with individual authority roles in
the professional sphere; formal rank receives emphasis as the
basis for effective control relationships in one context while
professional competence is emphasized in another context;
specialization and division of labor occur generally but not
particularly in connection with administrative work.

Since the organization under review was academic as
well as medical, it is not surprising that the net result of
this interweaving appears to approximate the semi-bureaucratic

pattern that Logan Wilson found to be more or less characteristic of faculties in American universities.[1] In outlining this type of structure he attended mainly -- though not exclusively -- to the locus of control, and thus placed semi-bureaucracy somewhere between the "company of equals" pattern and the hierarchical authority pattern described by Weber as characteristic of bureaucracy. Recognized but given less systematic attention by Wilson were possible variations in the type of control exercised within a semi-bureaucratic framework, as well as the question of how such types might vary in predictable ways according to the area of work considered.[2] Yet in characterizing an organization of professionals, the present analysis suggests that these dimensions also need to be considered explicitly.

In this connection, Gouldner's analysis of patterns of bureaucracy[3] provides a useful extension of Weber's work, and though he apparently did not intend it specifically as such, of Wilson's as well. On the basis of his examination of work relationships among the personnel in an indus... ...ich

---

[1] Op. cit., pp. 79-82.

[2] Wilson was not, of course, alone ... ... these factors; virtually everyone who has at ... ...ation of professionals who work in organi... ...ed that control relationships with regard to ... ... must differ from bureaucratic auth... ... ...specif... ing logical and feasible org... ... ..., however, analysts appear to have been ... ... by ... ... to see all aspects of the expert's wor... ... ...io... ... ...indi- vidualism as the only alterna...ive ... ...e auth...r...y.

[3] Alvin W. Gouldner, op. cit., ...

mined and processed gypsum, Gouldner differentiated three patterns of bureaucracy: "mock," "representative" and "punishment-
centered." All three types involve division of labor, a hierarchy of positions, and rules; what distinguishes one type from
another are not these gross bureaucratic features but the relative presence or absence of particular sets of conditions within this broad framework. As Gouldner indicates, in mock
bureaucracy, rules are neither enforced by those in superordinate positions nor obeyed by those in subordinate positions; joint violation and evasion of rules is buttressed by
the informal sentiments of participants; and as a consequence,
there is usually little conflict between the two groups. In
punishment-centered bureaucracy, however, rules are either enforced by those in superordinate positions or those in subordinate positions, and evaded by the other; enforcement occurs
through punishment and is supported by the informal sentiments
of either the superordinate or subordinate group; consequently
relatively great tension and conflict is entailed. Finally, in
representative bureaucracy rules are both enforced by those in
superordinate positions and obeyed by those in subordinate
positions; there is joint support for the rules, buttressed by
informal sentiments, mutual participation, initiation, and education of those in both groups; and as a result, a few tensions
but little overt conflict occur.[1]

---

[1] These descriptions represent slight paraphrases of
those presented by Gouldner, ibid., p. 217.

In discussing the relative prevalence of the representative pattern as compared with the punishment-centered pattern, Gouldner suggests that "it may be wise to adopt the working hypothesis that representative bureaucracy in _industrial_ settings operates in a 'social space' whose contours, opportunities, and barriers are defined and shaped by punishment-centered bureaucracy."[1] It may, however, be equally wise to apply this hypothesis in reverse to academic and other professional work settings. For of the three types, it is representative bureaucracy that, more than the other two, appears to specify further what Wilson meant by a semi-bureaucratic pattern and, at the same time, to portray in part the sort of organization that has been under analysis in the present study. In addition, however, to anticipating that representative bureaucracy will be more prevalent among professionals than will the punishment-centered type, proposed here is the co-existence and relatively high prevalence among professionals of a fourth type of pattern: _advisory_ bureaucracy.

This type does not involve, as do the three outlined by Goulder, organizational "rules" that are "enforced" or "unenforced" by those in charge, or that are "obeyed" or "evaded" by those in subordinate positions. Rather than rules, specific technical knowledge and guiding principles for the application of this knowledge represent the content-focus of advisory

---

[1]Ibid., pp. 224-25. (Underlining supplied.)

bureaucracy. Further, in advisory bureaucracy the counterpart
of enforcement of rules is the formal obligation to give advice
based on technical knowledge, while the counterpart of obedi-
ence is the obligation to take such advice under critical
review when making relevant decisions.

The advisory pattern is similar to representative
bureaucracy, however, in that it is responsible for some tensions but little conflict between those in charge and those in
subordinate positions. Factors associated with the avoidance
of conflict would also seem to be similar to those which
Gouldner suggests[1] are involved in representative bureaucracy.
That is, the body of technical knowledge and principles for
application are shared by both groups and legitimated by their
values; the advisory relationship does not violate either
group's values; deviance from accepted technical principles is
viewed as correctable through education instead of punishment,
since it is seen as a result of ignorance or accident rather
than willful error; and finally, such deviance impairs the
status of both superordinates and subordinates, while conformity either maintains or improves the status of both.

In short, the advisory pattern has much in common with
the representative pattern so far as certain hypothesized
social and cultural antecedents, correlates, and consequences
are concerned. Indeed, there is reason to believe that in

[1]Ibid., pp. 216-17.

organizations of professionals, the two patterns may necessarily supplement each other, as has been suggested was the
case in the CC&TP. Gouldner, however, was not faced with an
organization composed primarily of professionals, but rather
with an organization in which trained experts were few and
unusual; in outlining bureaucratic patterns, therefore, he
understandably overlooked the possibility of a formal hierarchy
of influence that might parallel and be functionally associated
with a formal hierarchy of authority.

To suggest that there is a type of bureaucratic pattern
that involves neither hierarchical authority nor specific rules
may appear to be a contradiction in terms, in that, following
Weber, these features have often been considered defining characteristics of bureaucratic organization. However, the bureaucracy that Weber describes is an ideal type, which, as Blau has
recently and cogently pointed out, "includes not only defini-
tions of concepts but also generalizations about the relationships between them, specifically the hypothesis that the diverse bureaucratic characteristics increase administrative
efficiency. Whether strict hierarchical authority, for example,
in fact furthers efficiency is a question of empirical fact and
not one of definition."[1]   On the basis of such reasoning, the
advisory pattern here outlined qualifies for at least provisional inclusion as one of the complex sets of factors that

---

[1]Peter M. Blau, Bureaucracy in Modern Society, p. 34.

may, under certain circumstances, promote efficiency in
achieving organizational aims.

Certainly, it has not been empirically demonstrated
that the pattern is inefficient, especially in organizations
such as universities, hospitals, and research units, where the
presence of professionals is required in order to fulfill adequately the organization's objectives. More generally, the
organizational functions and dysfunctions of the advisory pattern remain largely unexplored, and it is only in the light of
empirical investigation of these matters that sound conclusions
could be drawn concerning the pattern's efficiency or ineffi-
ciency.

Thus whether the pattern is called a type of bureaucracy, an aspect of semi-bureaucracy, or something else entirely
would seem to be less important, in the long run, than its
identification as a probable characteristic of professional
staff organization whose prevalence, antecedents, correlates,
and consequences require further empirical research and analysis. In this respect, comparative studies of organized professional staffs are clearly necessary.

The Problem of Explanation

Comparative studies are also necessary in order to
clarify the conditions which determine whether one or another
type of organizational pattern will prevail among physicians as
well as among other professionals. How does it happen, for
example, that both advisory and representative bureaucracy were

institutionalized among physicians in the CC&TF, while among
physicians in Soviet Russia, these patterns were evidently considerably less prevalent than punishment-centered bureaucracy?
What conditions explain the variety of patterns which, according to Logan Wilson, organizations of academicians may display?
Obviously, this problem is closely related to the problem of
accounting for the differential impact which professional norms
and values may have in shaping the organizational roles of professionals. Why, for instance, were professional pressures
effective in the CC&TP and, apparently, not so effective in the
Sick Fund of the General Federation of Labor in Israel, or in
the labor unions described by Wilensky? More generally, assuming that, by reason of their intensive training, professionals
are equally motivated to live up to professional role prescrip-
tions and to mold their organizational roles accordingly, what
circumstances permit or prevent them from doing so?

These questions are raised primarily to indicate a
potentially fruitful area for future research. For clearly,
adequate answers are not at hand, partly because the several
studies cited do not focus to the same extent on possible ex-
planatory factors that may be compared, and partly because the
general problem itself is in only a rudimentary state of sociological analysis. That is, it seems highly likely that differences in such conditions as the relative number, formal power
position, informal bargaining power, prestige, indispensability,
degree of professionalization, and potential or actual

alternative careers of professional persons may help account
for observed differences in their organizational roles. But
how these and other factors -- such as organizational objectives, incentives, and sanctions -- may combine dynamically to
produce specific role differences as well as particular types
of bureaucratic patterns among professionals is not at all
clear, even on the level of systematic speculation.

Lipset's incisive discussion of the analytic and methodological difficulties involved in accounting for differences
in the structure of trade unions is equally applicable and in-
structive in the present context:

> Clearly, it is impossible in the case of given
> organizations or individuals to abstract any one
> variable and make it the sole or even primary
> determinant of a given behavior pattern. The
> problem of how to deal with multi-factored de-
> terminants of specific behavior patterns is a
> basic one in the social sciences. When dealing
> with individuals, analysts may partially escape
> the difficulty by collecting data on a large
> number of cases, so that they can isolate the
> influence of specific factors through use of
> quantitative techniques. The analysis of
> organizations is hampered, however, by the fact
> that comparable data are rarely collected for
> more than a few cases. The cost of studying
> intensively even one large organization may be
> as much as that of gathering survey data from a
> large sample of individuals.
>
> The usual procedure followed by most analysts in
> searching out the determinants of a given pattern
> of behavior, such as oligarchy or rank and file
> militancy within a given labor union, is to cite
> those factors present in the organization which
> seem to be related to the behavioral item in
> question. Such a procedure is essentially post
> factum, however, if the only case in which the
> given pattern of significant variables is ob-
> served is the one under observation. The analyst

rarely has the opportunity to establish any controls or comparisons. Often an attempt is made
to escape this dilemma by citing illustrative
materials from other cases, which appear to validate the hypothesis. Such illustrative data do
not solve the methodological problem of valida-
tion, and usually only serve to give the reader
a false sense of the general validity of the
interpretation.

It is of crucial importance, therefore, that
students of organizational behavior address themselves to the problem of verification of hypotheses. At the present time, one may spend a great
deal of time examining the large number of
studies of individual trade unions or other
large-scale organizations without being able to
validate a single proposition about organizational behavior. The data collected in such
case studies do not lend themselves to re-analy-
sis to test hypotheses, since the researchers
rarely focused their observations in terms of
any set of explicit hypotheses.

Three methods may be tentatively suggested as
ways through which greater progress can be made
in this area: the gathering of quantitative data
from a large number of organizations, clinical
case studies, and deviant case analyses.[1]

All three of the research methods cited by Lipset --

the quantitative survey, the case study, and analysis of devi-

ant cases -- could be used profitably by sociologists of the

professions to explore systematically the factors which lead to

various types of organization among professionals, as well as

to investigate the nature and prevalence of the types them-

selves more thoroughly than has yet been done. Perhaps a

---

[1]Seymour Martin Lipset, "The Political Process in Trade
Unions: A Theoretical Statement," in Morroe Berger, Theodore
Abel, and Charles H. Page (eds.), Freedom and Control in Modern
Society (New York: Van Nostrand Co., 1954), pp. 82-124, at pp.
122-23. (Underlining supplied.)

measure of what remains to be accomplished is the fact that
currently, with respect to physicians as well as other professionals who work in organized settings, it is impossible to
indicate with any degree of empirical certainty what type of
organization constitutes a "deviant case" and what type is
modal.

Additional Directions for Research

Not considered explicitly in this study but no less
worthy of research are a number of other, more or less related,
problems.

In focusing on the formal structure of role relationships among physicians in the CC&TP, for example, this study
has essentially ignored the informal dimension: the network of
interpersonal relationships represented by friendship, enmity,
or indifference that, as analysts of other organizational settings have shown, always arise and frequently affect role behavior in work situations. How such informal, affective ties
condition the exercise and acceptance of formal supervision
among physicians, particularly with respect to their professional work, must nevertheless eventually receive investigative
attention if control relationships among these professionals
are to be fully understood.

Moreover, although this study has dealt exclusively
with relatively explicit modes of control among physicians, the
existence of less explicit, more indirect means must also be
recognized and their influence on professional behavior

assessed. For example, some hospitals -- and all medical schools -- conduct regular clinical-pathological conferences, in which staff diagnoses made on the basis of clinical evidence are compared with those that emerge from post-mortem, laboratory examination of a recently deceased patient. While such conferences are not formally viewed as a mechanism for controlling the professional behavior of staff physicians, it seems exceedingly likely that, through demonstrating areas of uncertainty, ignorance, and error, they function ultimately in a control capacity. Likewise, the academic milieu in general and the presence of medical students in particular may serve as indirect control mechanisms. In supervising the diagnostic and therapeutic work that students do, staff physicians are sometimes challenged to justify their opinions and advice by students who are otherwise convinced, and their professional decisions are often subject to the informal scrutiny of students and staff alike. Physicians may, therefore, consciously or unconsciously be somewhat more rigorous and careful in their standards of patient care than would otherwise occur.

Apart from the matter of identifying various types of indirect organizational mechanisms for controlling professional conduct, there is the broad problem of delineating the socialization process through which physicians acquire their expectations concerning professional independence, supervision, and

consultation.[1] The present study investigated the expectations
of physicians in the advanced years of residency training and
beyond; what these expectations were at earlier stages of their
training would, however, be worth knowing, since changes in
expectations -- and the experiences that produce them -- constitute significant milestones in the socialization process.

---

[1]The program of sociological research on medical education and professional socialization that is in progress at the
Bureau of Applied Social Research, Columbia University, may be
expected to throw some light on the development of these expectations. For some preliminary reports, see Robert K. Merton,
George G. Reader, and Patricia L. Kendall, op. cit.

APPENDIX A

QUESTIONNAIRE USED TO OBTAIN INFORMATION FROM FACULTY MEMBERS

AT CORNELL UNIVERSITY MEDICAL COLLEGE, 1956: PREPARED

BY DAVID CAPLOVITZ

BUREAU OF APPLIED SOCIAL RESEARCH

Columbia University

STUDIES IN MEDICAL EDUCATION

Opinions of Faculty Members at
Cornell University Medical College

To Members of Cornell Medical College Faculty:

This questionnaire represents one part of a continuing study of
medical education being conducted by the Bureau of Applied
Social Research. In other phases of the study we have examined
the attitudes of medical students. We are now focusing upon
the opinions of clinical faculty members.

The questions relate to matters of medical education and medical care. We recognize that some questions deal with complex
issues and that the check list alternatives do not always express the subtleties of your opinions. But the aim of a questionnaire like this is to obtain an overall picture of the
attitudes of the faculty and for this purpose check list alternatives are most appropriate.

Some of you may feel that because of your limited contacts with
students you are not fully qualified to answer all of the questions. However, in order to insure the success of this study
it is important that all clinical faculty members--no matter
how little time they devote to teaching--fill out and return
the questionnaire.

Your personal answers will be kept in strictest confidence. No
member of the faculty or administration of Cornell Medical College will see your questionnaire. The information will be tab-
ulated by the Bureau of Applied Social Research and made available only in the form of statistical summaries. However, you
are asked to sign your name in the space provided below in
order that we may know which questionnaires have been returned.
Your signature will be detached as soon as your questionnaire
is received.

We thank you in advance for the time and thought you will give
to this questionnaire. Any comments you wish to make may be
recorded in the space provided at the end. When you are
finished, please mail it to us in the enclosed envelope as soon
as possible.

(Please print your name here)

172

THESE QUESTIONS DEAL WITH YOUR EVALUATIONS OF CERTAIN QUALITIES AND BEHAVIOR IN CLINICAL STUDENTS.

1. Below is a list of 14 problems and situations which Cornell medical students occasionally meet in their clinical years. How much competence do you think third and fourth year students at Cornell should have in dealing with each of these situations? (Please answer in terms of your standards of competence even if the students you have observed do not conform with them.)

Fill in the blanks with appropriate numbers from the following code:

1 - Should be completely competent
2 - Should be fairly competent
3 - Cannot expect him to be really competent
4 - Cannot expect him to be able to handle situation at all

EXAMPLE:

	Student at end of 3rd year	Student at end of 4th year
Taking a patient's temperature...	1	1

This means that in the matter of taking a patient's temperature you think that third year and fourth year students should have the same degree of competence, in this instance, complete competence.

	Student at end of 3rd year	Student at end of 4th year
1) The patient who has an emotional outburst of some kind............	___(25)	___(26)
2) Preventing a patient from becoming embarrassed during a pelvic examination......................	___(27)	___(28)
3) Having to do a painful procedure on a sick child..................	___(29)	___(30)
4) Deciding what to tell a patient who has a serious and irremediable problem........................	___(31)	___(32)

	Student at end of 3rd year	Student at end of 4th year
5) Knowing what to do in an emergency.........................	__(33)	__(34)
6) Being able to do a venipuncture without any difficulty...........	__(35)	__(36)
7) Having to tell a patient that the tests performed on him do not reveal the cause of his problems..	__(37)	__(38)
8) Having a doctor as one of his patients........................	__(39)	__(40)
9) Being able to make a diagnosis in a difficult case.................	__(41)	__(42)
10) Deciding on appropriate medication and dosage......................	__(43)	__(44)
11) Handling a patient who refuses to accept what the student tells him.	__(45)	__(46)
12) Diagnosing mitral stenosis by auscultation of the heart.........	__(47)	__(48)
13) Discussing the differential diagnosis of obstructive jaundice and hepatitis........................	__(49)	__(50)
14) Presenting a clinical case history.........................	__(51)	__(52)

2. How much importance do you personally attach to each of the following when judging the competence of clinical students and physicians in your specialty?

Fill in the blanks with appropriate numbers from the following code:

1 - Great importance
2 - Moderate importance
3 - Minor importance
4 - No importance

	Student at end of 3rd year	Student at end of 4th year	Physician in your specialty
a)			
1) Extensive knowledge of medical facts............	___(15)	___(16)	___(17)
2) Ability to get along with other students or colleagues...............	___(18)	___(19)	___(20)
3) Ability to get along with the faculty..............	___(21)	___(22)	
4) Ability to put aside everything but medicine..	___(23)	___(24)	___(25)
5) Ability to carry out research.................	___(26)	___(27)	___(28)
6) Skill in the realm of diagnosis................	___(29)	___(30)	___(31)
7) Ability to establish rapport with patients....	___(32)	___(33)	___(34)
8) Ability to work effectively with nurses and technicians..............	___(35)	___(36)	___(37)
9) Knowledge of therapy.....	___(38)	___(39)	___(40)
10) Skill in dealing with the social and psychological problems of patients.....	___(41)	___(42)	___(43)
11) Knowledge of community agencies of help in the care of patients........	___(44)	___(45)	___(46)

b) Which one of the above qualities do you personally consider most important when judging third year students, fourth year students and physicians in your specialty? (Please answer below on the left.)

Which one of the above do you consider least important? (Answer below on the right.)

MOST IMPORTANT   LEAST IMPORTANT

#___(47)   In judging third year students.   #___(50)
#___(48)   In judging fourth year students.   #___(51)
#___(49)   In judging physicians in your   #___(52)
              specialty.

c) Are there any qualities not mentioned above which you consider of particular importance when judging students or physicians? What?

3. How would you feel if a third year student, fourth year student, and physician in your specialty were to do each of the following:

Fill in the blanks with appropriate numbers from the following code:

1 - Would disapprove strongly
2 - Would disapprove to some extent
3 - Would not care
4 - Would approve mildly
5 - Would approve strongly

	Student at end of 3rd year	Student at end of 4th year	Physician in your specialty
1) Express a desire to discharge from care a patient with a functional problem.	___(15)	___(16)	___(17)
2) Question his instructor's judgment with respect to a clinical problem..........	___(18)	___(19)	
3) Admit his uncertainties with respect to a diagnostic problem............	___(20)	___(21)	___(22)
4) Spend a lot of time exploring social and emotional factors when taking a history................	___(23)	___(24)	___(25)
5) Show little or no interest in patients with routine medical problems..........	___(26)	___(27)	___(28)
6) Spend more than an hour and a half working up a patient...................	___(29)	___(30)	___(31)
7) Advise patients on their personal problems.........	___(32)	___(33)	___(34)
8 Wait for the instructor to set up the plan of treatment for a patient..........	___(35)	___(36)	

	Student at end of 3rd year	Student at end of 4th year	Physician in your specialty
9) Always tell patients the full extent of their illness..................	___(37)	___(38)	___(39)
10) Be an "eager beaver"; always do more than is requested...............	___(40)	___(41)	
11) Make a diagnosis of psychoneurosis without first ordering all possible tests to rule out organic factors..................	___(42)	___(43)	___(44)
12) Admit to being moved by a particular patient.......	___(45)	___(46)	___(47)

4. What is your best guess as to how most third and fourth year students would answer the previous question? That is, how would they feel if a fellow student were to do each of the following:

Fill in the blanks with appropriate numbers from the following code:

1 - Would disapprove strongly
2 - Would disapprove to some extent
3 - Would not care
4 - Would approve mildly
5 - Would approve strongly

	How most 3rd year students would feel if a classmate were to:	How most 4th year students would feel if a classmate were to:
1) Express a desire to discharge from care a patient with a functional problem...	___(48)	___(49)
2) Question his instructor's judgment with respect to a clinical problem...........	___(50)	___(51)
3) Admit his uncertainties with respect to a diagnostic problem....................	___(52)	___(53)

	How most 3rd year students would feel if a classmate were to:	How most 4th year students would feel if a classmate were to:
4) Spend a lot of time exploring social and emotional factors when taking a history...	___(54)	___(55)
5) Show little or no interest in patients with routine medical problems............	___(56)	___(57)
6) Spend more than an hour and a half working up a patient..	___(58)	___(59)
7) Advise patients on their personal problems............	___(60)	___(61)
8) Wait for the instructor to set up the plan of treatment for a patient................	___(62)	___(63)
9) Always tell patients the full extent of their illness......	___(64)	___(65)
10) Be an "eager beaver"; always do more than is required.....	___(66)	___(67)
11) Make a diagnosis of psychoneurosis without first ordering all possible tests to rule out organic factors.....	___(68)	___(69)
12) Admit to being moved by a particular patient..........	___(70)	___(71)

5. These questions deal with some aspects of the clinical teaching program at Cornell. Please answer each question as it applies to the third year and then as it applies to the fourth year.

a) What is your feeling about the amount of responsibility students taking courses in your department have with regard to diagnosis?

	3rd year (Check one)	4th year (Check one)
They have too much responsibility..	___15-1	___ 5
They do not have enough responsibility................	___ 2	___ 6
They have about the right amount of responsibility.............	___ 3	___ 7

b) What about the amount of responsibility students taking courses in your department have with regard to <u>treatment</u>?

	3rd year (Check one)	4th year (Check one)
They have too much responsibility...	16-1	5
They do not have enough responsibility...................	2	6
They have about the right amount of responsibility................	3	7

c) All things considered do you think that clinical students at Cornell receive

	3rd year (Check one)	4th year (Check one)
Too much direction and guidance.....	17-1	5
Not enough direction and guidance...	2	6
About the right amount of direction and guidance.....................	3	7

d) What about the kinds of patients clinical students should see? Do you think they should see "hand picked" patients or do you think they should see a representative sample of patients?

	3rd year (Check one)	4th year (Check one)
"Hand picked".......................	18-1	4
Representative sample...............	2	5

e) Do you think clinical students profit more from

	3rd year (Check one)	4th year (Check one)
seeing as many new patients as possible even at the expense of following old patients...........	7	0
seeing fewer new patients and following the patients they do see......................	8	X

f) Do you think that giving clinical students the opportunity to learn how to handle the social and psychological problems of their patients

	3rd year (Check one)	4th year (Check one)
Helps them to acquire technical medical knowledge..............	19-1	5

Hinders their acquiring technical
medical knowledge............... ___ 2   ___ 6
Has no effect on their acquiring
technical medical knowledge..... ___ 3   ___ 7

g) Do you think clinical students should make some home visits
(under supervision) in order to observe the patient's
family and home environment or do you think this time would
be more profitably spent in other activities?

	3rd year (Check one)	4th year (Check one)
They should make some home visits for this reason...............	___20-1	___ 4
This time would be more profitably spent in other activities.......	___ 2	___ 5

h) Do you think there should be more emphasis at Cornell on
training students as general physicians or do you think
there should be less emphasis on this kind of training?

There should be more emphasis on
this kind of training...........   ___ 7
There should be less emphasis on
this kind of training...........   ___ 8
The present emphasis is about
right..........................   ___ 9

6. In recent years several new programs have been introduced in
the curriculum at Cornell. Among these have been Medical
Education for National Defense (M.E.N.D.) and the Comprehensive Care and Teaching Program. Please answer the following
questions for each of these programs. (The left hand column
is for M.E.N.D. and the right hand column is for the Comprehensive Care and Teaching Program.)

Medical Education for National Defense (Check one)		Comprehensive Care and Teaching Program (Check one)
	a) How much do you know about each of these programs?	
21-1___	Quite a bit........................	___23-1
2___	Not very much......................	___ 2
3___	Nothing at all.....................	___ 3

b) Check the statement which comes closest
to expressing your overall opinion of
each program

Check one   Check one

5___   1) I think that in principle the program
          is a good idea, and that in general
          it has worked out very well.........   ___ 5

6___   2) I think that in principle the program
          is a good idea, but that it has not
          worked out as well as it might have.. ___ 6

7___   3) I am not particularly in sympathy
          with the principles of the program,
          but it has worked out better than I
          would have expected..................   ___ 7

8___   4) I am not particularly in sympathy
          with the principles of the program,
          and as far as I can see, it has not
          worked out very well................   ___ 8

9___   5) I really don't know enough about the
          program to say......................   ___ 9

c) Would you recommend each of these
programs to other medical schools?

Check one   Check one

22-1___ Yes   Yes   ___ 24-1
   2___ No   No   ___   2
   3___ Don't know   Don't know ___ 3

7. Everyone recognizes that it is difficult to generalize about
the medical profession as a whole. But in your judgment
what is the average prestige that members of the medical
profession at large assign to each of the following types of
doctors?

Column 1 means very high prestige, column 5, very little
prestige. Columns 2, 3, and 4 represent gradations between
these extremes.

a) Rating by medical profession:

Answer for Each		Very high prestige 1	2	3	4	Very little prestige 5
Surgeons.............	(25)	—	—	—	—	—
General Practitioners	(26)	—	—	—	—	—
Pediatricians........	(27)	—	—	—	—	—
Psychiatrists........	(28)	—	—	—	—	—
Obstetricians........	(29)	—	—	—	—	—
Internists...........	(30)	—	—	—	—	—
Professors in a medical school....	(31)	—	—	—	—	—
Doctors in your specialty (if not one of above).....	(32)	—	—	—	—	—

b) How do you yourself rate each of these groups:

Answer for Each		Very high prestige 1	2	3	4	Very little prestige 5
Surgeons.............	(33)	—	—	—	—	—
General Practitioners	(34)	—	—	—	—	—
Pediatricians........	(35)	—	—	—	—	—
Psychiatrists........	(36)	—	—	—	—	—
Obstetricians........	(37)	—	—	—	—	—
Internists...........	(38)	—	—	—	—	—
Doctors in your specialty (if not one of above).....	(39)	—	—	—	—	—

FACTUAL INFORMATION

1. Sex: Male.................. 41-1
                                     Female............... ___ 2

2. Age: Under 35............. ___ 4
                                     35-45................ ___ 5
                                     46-55................ ___ 6
                                     Over 55.............. ___ 7

3. Department: Medicine............. 42-1
                                     Surgery.............. ___ 2
                                     Obstetrics and
                                       Gynecology........ ___ 3
                                     Pediatrics.......... ___ 4
                                     Psychiatry.......... ___ 5
                                     Public Health and
                                       Prevent. Med...... ___ 6
                                     Other............... ___ 7

   a) Name of specialty_____

   b) If you have an interest in a sub-specialty

      Name of sub-specialty_____
      Do not have sub-specialty_____ ___

4. Rank: Full Professor...... 45-1
                                     Associate Professor. ___ 2
                                     Assistant Professor. ___ 3
                                     Instructor.......... ___ 4
                                     Resident............ ___ 5
                                     Research Associate.. ___ 6

5. Type of Appointment: Full-time........... ___ 3
                                     Geographical
                                       full-time........ ___ 9
                                     Part-time........... ___ 0
                                     Resident............ ___ x
                                     Research Associate.. ___ y

   a) Do you have a private practice: Yes ___ 46-1
                                                       No ___ 2
     (IF NO) Have you ever had a
     private practice?   Yes ___ 4
                                                       No ___ 5

6. From which medical school were you graduated?_____

_____

7. Please rank the following activities in terms of the amount of time you spend on them. Please make a second ranking in terms of the amount of interest you have in them. (Place a 1 in front of the activity which takes most of your time, 2, next to the activity which takes the next largest amount of time, etc.)

Amount of TIME spent (Rank all five)		Amount of INTEREST (Rank all five)
(49)___	Seeing patients in private practice...............	___(54)
(50)___	Seeing patients in clinics or wards...............	___(55)
(51)___	Teaching.....................	___(56)
(52)___	Research.....................	___(57)
(53)___	Administration.............	___(58)

8. For about what proportion of the patients you see do you assume continuing responsibility for management?

	In private practice (check one)	At medical center (wards, clinics) (check one)
10% or less.................	__ 59-1	__ 60-1
About 25%..................	__ 2	__ 2
About half.................	__ 3	__ 3
About 75%..................	__ 4	__ 4
Almost all.................	__ 5	__ 5
Does not apply.............	__ 6	__ 6

9. Are you teaching Cornell undergraduate medical students this year (1955-'56)?............... Yes ___ 61-1   No ___ 2

Did you teach undergraduate medical students at Cornell last year (1954-'55)?........ Yes ___ 4   No ___ 5

Did you teach Cornell undergraduates during the year of 1953-'54?................... Yes ___ 7   No ___ 8

10. On the average, how many hours a week did you spend teaching Cornell undergraduate medical students during each of these years?

	1955-'56 (check one)	1954-'55 (check one)	1953-'54 (check one)
1-3 hours per week	62-1	7	63-1
4-10 hours per week	2	8	2
11-20 hours per week	3	9	3
More than 20 hours	4	0	4
Did not teach	5	x	5

11. Which classes of medical students did you teach in each of these years?

	1955-'56	1954-'55	1953-'54
First year class	64-1	7	65-1
Second year class	2	8	2
Third year class	3	9	3
Fourth year class	4	0	4
Did not teach	5	x	5

a) With which class did you spend most time?

	(66)	(67)	(68)
	(class)	(class)	(class)

12. What kind of teaching did you do primarily in each of these years?

	1955-'56 (check one)	1954-'55 (check one)	1953-'54 (check one)
Attending	69-1	6	70-1
Tutor	2	7	2
Lecturer	3	8	3
Did not teach	4	9	4

13. Where did you have most contact with students:

	1955-'56 (check one)	1954-'55 (check one)	1953-'54 (check one)
Wards	71-1	7	72-1
General clinics	2	8	2
Specialty clinics	3	9	3
Lecture room	4	0	4
Did not teach	5	x	5

14. On the average, about how many clinical students do you teach in the course of a year?

                3rd year students   4th year students

                     # ___   # ___

15. Would you please identify three or four outstanding students you have taught in the last three years who you think show promise of becoming particularly good physicians?

Name of Student	Year in which he was your student		
	1955-56	1954-55	1953-54
1. _____	___	___	___
2. _____	___	___	___
3. _____	___	___	___
4. _____	___	___	___

Any comments you wish to make may be recorded here.

APPENDIX B

SUPPLEMENTARY TABLES

TABLE A

JUDGMENTS OF MOST IMPORTANT QUALITY IN PROFESSIONAL COMPETENCE

Quality:	Physicians who Believe Quality is "MOST IMPORTANT" in Judging Competence of Colleague	
	Number	Per Cent
Skill in realm of diagnosis	235	49
Extensive knowledge of medical facts	80	17
Knowledge of therapy	64	13
Ability to establish rapport with patients	54	11
Skill in dealing with social and psychological problems of patients	25	5
Ability to get along with other colleagues	14	3
Ability to carry out research	6	1
Ability to put aside everything but medicine	5	1
Ability to work effectively with nurses and technicians	--	--
Knowledge of community agencies of help in the care of patients	--	--
Total	483[a]	100%

[a]This total omits those who did not answer the question.

TABLE B

JUDGMENTS OF MOST IMPORTANT QUALITY IN PROFESSIONAL COMPETENCE:
BY RANK

| Qualities: | Per Cent who Believe Quality is "MOST IMPORTANT" in Judging Competence of Colleague | | | |
	Full Prof. & Assoc. Prof.	Asst. Prof.	Instructor	Resident & Research Assoc.
Skill in realm of diagnosis	51%	54%	51%	50%
Extensive knowledge of medical facts	11	17	20	20
Knowledge of therapy	15	7	12	19
Ability to establish rapport with patients	9	11	10	8
Skill in dealing with social and psychological problems of patients	4	6	2	3
Other qualities	10	5	5	--
	100%	100%	100%	100%
Total number	(95)	(115)	(161)	(74)

TABLE C

JUDGMENTS OF MOST IMPORTANT QUALITY IN PROFESSIONAL COMPETENCE:
BY TYPE OF APPOINTMENT

Qualities:	Per Cent who Believe Quality is "MOST IMPORTANT" in Judging Competence of Colleague		
	Full-time	Part-time[a]	Residents and Research Assoc.
Skill in realm of diagnosis	51%	49%	40%
Extensive knowledge of medical facts	13	16	21
Knowledge of therapy	12	12	22
Ability to establish rapport with patients	13	11	13
Skill in dealing with social and psychological problems of patients	3	6	3
Other qualities	8	6	1
	100%	100%	100%
Total number	(76)	(335)	(72)

[a]Includes Geographic Full-time faculty members.

BIBLIOGRAPHY

BIBLIOGRAPHY

Books:

Argyris, Chris. Diagnosing Human Relations in Organizations: a Case Study of a Hospital. New Haven: Labor and Management Center, Yale University, 1956.

Bachman, George W., and Associates. Health Resources in the United States: Personnel, Facilities, and Services. Washington, D.C.: The Brookings Institution, 1952.

Barber, Bernard. Science and the Social Order. Glencoe, Ill.: The Free Press, 1952.

Barnard, Chester I. The Functions of the Executive. Cambridge: Harvard University Press, 1938.

Blau, Peter M. The Dynamics of Bureaucracy. Chicago: The University of Chicago Press, 1955.

Blau, Peter M. Bureaucracy in Modern Society. New York: Random House, 1956.

Burling, Temple, Lentz, Edith M., and Wilson, Robert N. The Give and Take in Hospitals. New York: G.P. Putnam's Sons, 1956.

Caplow, Theodore. The Sociology of Work. Minneapolis: University of Minnesota Press, 1954.

Carr-Saunders, A.M., and Wilson, P.A. The Professions. Oxford: Clarendon Press, 1933.

Cornell University Medical College. Announcement for 1953-54 Sessions. Ithaca: Cornell University, 1953.

Davis, Kingsley. Human Society. New York: The Macmillan Co., 1948.

Deitrick, John E., and Berson, Robert C. Medical Schools in the United States at Mid-Century. New York: McGraw-Hill Book Co., Inc., 1953.

Dubin, Robert. Human Relations in Administration. New York: Prentice-Hall, Inc., 1951.

Durkheim, Emile. The Division of Labor in Society. Tr. by George Simpson, Glencoe, Ill.: The Free Press, 1949.

Field, Mark G. Doctor and Patient in Soviet Russia. Cambridge: Harvard University Press, 1957.

Francis, Roy G., and Stone, Robert C. Service and Procedure in Bureaucracy. Minneapolis: The University of Minnesota Press, 1956.

Garceau, Oliver. The Political Life of the American Medical Association. Cambridge: Harvard University Press, 1941.

Gerth, H.H., and Mills, C. Wright (tr.). From Max Weber: Essays in Sociology. New York: Oxford University Press, 1946.

Goode, William J., Merton, Robert K., and Huntington, Mary Jean. The Professions in American Society: A Sociological Analysis and Casebook. (Forthcoming)

Gouldner, Alvin W. (ed.). Studies in Leadership. New York: Harper and Bros., 1950.

Gouldner, Alvin W. Patterns of Industrial Bureaucracy. Glencoe, Ill.: The Free Press, 1954.

Greenblatt, Milton, Levinson, Daniel J., and Williams, Richard H. The Patient and the Mental Hospital. Glencoe, Ill.: The Free Press, 1957.

Gulick, Luther, and Urwick, L. Papers on the Science of Administration. New York: Institute of Public Administration, 1937.

Henderson, A.M., and Parsons, Talcott (tr.). Max Weber: The Theory of Social and Economic Organization. New York: Oxford University Press, 1947.

Hospital Council of Greater New York. Hospital Staff Appointments of Physicians in New York City. New York: The Macmillan Co., 1951.

Jahoda, Marie, Deutsch, Morton, and Cook, Stuart W. Research Methods in Social Relations. New York: The Dryden Press, 1951.

Katz, Elihu, and Lazarsfeld, Paul F. Personal Influence. Glencoe, Ill.: The Free Press, 1955.

Kingsley, J. Donald. Representative Bureaucracy. Yellow Springs, Ohio: Antioch Press, 1944.

Lazarsfeld, Paul F., and Thielens, Wagner, Jr. The Academic Mind: Social Scientists in a Time of Crisis. (in press)

Lewis, Roy, and Maude, Angus. Professional People in England. Cambridge: Harvard University Press, 1952.

Lipset, Seymour M. Agrarian Socialism. Berkeley: University of California Press, 1950.

Lipset, Seymour M., Trow, Martin A., and Coleman, James S. Union Democracy. Glencoe, Ill.: The Free Press, 1956.

MacEachern, Malcolm T. Hospital Organization and Management. Rev. third ed. Chicago: Physicians Record Co., 1957.

Merton, Robert K. Social Theory and Social Structure. Revised and enlarged ed. Glencoe, Ill.: The Free Press, 1957.

Merton, Robert K., Gray, Ailsa P., Hockey, Barbara, and Selvin, Hanan C. Reader in Bureaucracy. Glencoe, Ill.: The Free Press, 1952.

Merton, Robert K., Reader, George G., and Kendall, Patricia L. (eds.). The Student-Physician. Cambridge: Harvard University Press, 1957.

Metcalf, Henry G., and Urwick, L. (eds.). Dynamic Administration: The Collected Papers of Mary Parker Follett. New York: Harper, 1940.

Mills, C. Wright. White Collar. New York: Oxford University Press, 1951.

Moore, Wilbert E. Industrial Relations and the Social Order. Revised ed. New York: The Macmillan Co., 1951.

Park, Robert E., and Burgess, Ernest W. Introduction to the Science of Sociology. Second ed. Chicago: University of Chicago Press, 1924.

Parsons, Talcott. The Structure of Social Action. Glencoe, Ill.: The Free Press, 1949.

Parsons, Talcott. Essays in Sociological Theory: Pure and Applied. Glencoe, Ill.: The Free Press, 1949.

Parsons, Talcott. The Social System. Glencoe, Ill.: The Free Press, 1951.

Ponton, Thomas R. The Medical Staff in the Hospital. Chicago: Physicians' Record Co., Second ed., 1953.

Robinson, G. Canby. Adventures in Medical Education. Cambridge: Harvard University Press, 1957.

Selznick, Philip. TVA and the Grass Roots. Berkeley: University of California Press, 1953.

Selznick, Philip. Leadership in Administration. Evanston, Ill.: Row, Peterson and Co., 1957.

Shryock, Richard H. The Development of Modern Medicine. New York: Alfred A. Knopf, 1947.

Simon, Herbert A. Administrative Behavior. New York: The Macmillan Co., 1947.

Stanton, A.H., and Schwartz, M.H. The Mental Hospital. New York: Basic Books Inc., 1954.

Stern, Bernhard J. American Medical Practice in the Perspectives of a Century. Cambridge: Harvard University Press, 1945.

Stevenson, George S. (ed.). Administrative Medicine. New York: Josiah Macy, Jr. Foundation, 1955.

The Society of the New York Hospital. Annual Report for the Year 1953. New York: The Society of the New York Hospital, 1954.

Whyte, William Foote. Street Corner Society. Enlarged ed. Chicago: University of Chicago Press, 1955.

Wilensky, Harold L. Intellectuals in Labor Unions. Glencoe, Ill.: The Free Press, 1956.

Wilson, Logan. The Academic Man. New York: Oxford University Press, 1942.

Wolff, Kurt H. (Tr. and Ed.). The Sociology of Georg Simmel. Glencoe, Ill.: The Free Press, 1950.

Zetterberg, Hans L. (ed.). Sociology in the United States of America. Paris: UNESCO, 1956.

Articles, Monographs, and Pamphlets:

American Medical Association. "Principles of Medical Ethics," Chicago: American Medical Association, 1957.

Anon. "The American Medical Association: Power, Purpose, and Politics in Organized Medicine," Yale Law Journal, Vol. 63, No. 7 (May, 1954), pp. 937-1022.

Barr, David P. "The Teaching of Preventive Medicine," Journal of Medical Education, Vol. 28, No. 3 (March, 1953), pp. 49-56.

Barr, David P. "Extramural Facilities in Medical Education," Journal of Medical Education, Vol. 28, No. 7 (July, 1953), pp. 9-12.

Barrabee, Paul. "A Study of a Mental Hospital," Unpublished Ph.D. dissertation, Harvard University, 1951.

Becker, Howard, and Geer, Blanche. "Participant Observation and Interviewing: A Comparison," Human Organization, Vol. 16, No. 3 (Fall, 1957), pp. 28-32.

Ben-David, Joseph. "The Professional Role of the Physician in Bureaucratized Medicine: A Study in Role Conflict." (mineographed, 1957)

Bendix, Reinhard. "Bureaucracy: the Problem and its Setting," American Sociological Review, Vol. 12, No. 5 (October, 1947), pp. 493-507.

Bierstedt, Robert. "An Analysis of Social Power," American Sociological Review, Vol. 15, No. 6 (December, 1950), pp. 730-38.

Bierstedt, Robert. "The Problem of Authority" in Berger, M., Abel, T. and Page, C.H. (eds.), Freedom and Control in Modern Society, New York: D. Van Nostrand Co., Inc., 1954, pp. 67-81.

Blau, Peter M. "Formal Organization: Dimensions of Analysis," American Journal of Sociology, Vol. 63, No. 1 (July, 1957), pp. 58-69.

Brown, Paula. "Bureaucracy in a Government Laboratory," Social Forces, Vol. 32, No. 3 (March, 1954), pp. 259-68.

Bryson, Lyman. "Notes on a Theory of Advice," in Merton, R.K., et al., Reader in Bureaucracy, Glencoe, Ill.: The Free Press, 1952, pp. 202-16.

Bureau of Applied Social Research. "Master Card Codebook for the First Eight Groups to Go Through the Cornell Comprehensive Care and Teaching Program: Classes of 1953-1956," November, 1956 (dittoed).

Caplovitz, David. "Value-Orientations of Medical Students and Faculty Members," Paper delivered at the American Sociological Society Meetings, Washington, D.C., 1957 (dittoed).

Carr-Saunders, A.M., and Wilson, P.A. "Professions," Encyclopedia of the Social Sciences. Vol. 12, pp. 476-50.

Caudill, William. "Applied Anthropology in Medicine," in Kroeber, A.L. (ed.), Anthropology Today, Chicago: University of Chicago Press, 1953, pp. 771-807.

Coleman, James, and Katz, Elihu. "The Diffusion of an Innovation among Physicians," Sociometry, Vol. 20, No. 4 (December, 1957), pp. 253-70.

Comprehensive Care and Teaching Program. "Annual Reports," 1952-57 (mimeographed).

Coser, Rose Laub. "Authority and Decision-Making in a Hospital," American Sociological Review, Vol. 23, No. 1 (February, 1958), pp. 56-63.

Dickinson, Frank G. Distribution of Medical School Alumni in the United States as of April, 1950. Bulletin 101, Bureau of Medical Economic Research, A.M.A., Chicago: American Medical Association, 1956.

Festinger, Leon. "An Analysis of Compliant Behavior," in Sherif, Muzafer, and Wilson, M.O., Group Relations at the Crossroads, New York: Harper, 1953, pp. 232-56.

Field, Mark G. "Structured Strain in the Role of the Soviet Physician," American Journal of Sociology, Vol. 53, No. 5 (March, 1953), pp. 493-502.

Fox, Renee C. "Physicians and Patients on a Research Ward: A Study of Stress and Ways of Coming to Terms with Stress," Unpublished Ph.D. Dissertation, Radcliffe College, Harvard University, 1953.

Fox, Renee C. "A Sociological Calendar of Medical School," Working Paper in the Sociology of Medicine, Bureau of Applied Social Research, Columbia University, 1955-56 (dittoed).

Fox, Renee C. "Training for Uncertainty," in Merton, R.K., Reader, G.G., and Kendall, P.L., The Student-Physician, Cambridge: Harvard University Press, 1957, pp. 207-41.

Freeman, Howard E., and Reeder, Leo G. "Medical Sociology: a Review of the Literature," American Sociological Review, Vol. 22, No. 1 (Feb., 1957), pp. 73-81.

Goldhamer, H., and Shils, E.A. "Types of Power and Status," American Journal of Sociology, Vol. 45, No. 2 (Sept., 1939), pp. 171-78.

Goldstein, Bernard. "Some Aspects of the Nature of Unionism among Salaried Professionals in Industry," American Sociological Review, Vol. 20, No. 2 (April, 1955), pp. 199-205.

Goode, William J. "Community within a Community: The Professions," American Sociological Review, Vol. 22, No. 2 (April, 1957), pp. 194-200.

Goss, Mary E.W. "Change in the Cornell Comprehensive Care and Teaching Program," in Merton, R.K., Reader, G.G., and Kendall, P.L., The Student-Physician, Cambridge: Harvard University Press, 1957, pp. 249-70.

Goss, Mary E.W., and Reader, George G. "Collaboration between Sociologist and Physician," Social Problems, Vol. 4, No. 1 (July, 1956), pp. 82-89.

"Graduate Medical Education Issue," Journal of the American Medical Association, Vol. 165, No. 5 (Oct. 5, 1957).

Hall, Oswald. "The Informal Organization of the Medical Profession," Canadian Journal of Economics and Political Science, Vol. 12, No. 1 (Feb., 1946), pp. 30-44.

Hall, Oswald. "Stages of a Medical Career," American Journal of Sociology, Vol. 53, No. 5 (March, 1948), pp. 327-37.

Hall, Oswald. "Types of Medical Careers," American Journal of Sociology, Vol. 55, No. 3 (Nov., 1949), pp. 243-53.

Hall, Oswald. "Sociological Research in the Field of Medicine: Progress and Prospects," American Sociological Review, Vol. 16, No. 5 (Oct., 1951), pp. 639-43.

Hall, Oswald. "Some Problems in the Provision of Medical Service," Canadian Journal of Economics and Political Science, Vol. 20, No. 4 (Nov., 1954), pp. 456-66.

"Hospital Statistics," Hospitals, Vol. 32, No. 15 (August 1, 1958), Part II.

Hughes, Everett C. "Personality Types and the Division of Labor," American Journal of Sociology, Vol. 33, No. 5 (Mar., 1928), pp. 754-55.

Hughes, Everett C. "Institutional Office and the Person," American Journal of Sociology, Vol. 43, No. 3 (Nov., 1937), pp. 404-13.

Hughes, Everett C. "Dilemmas and Contradictions of Status," American Journal of Sociology, Vol. 50, No. 5 (Mar., 1945), pp. 353-59.

Hughes, Everett C. "Work and the Self," in Rohrer, J.H., and
    Serif, M. (ed.), Social Psychology at the Crossroads, New
    York: Harper and Bros., 1951, pp. 313-23.

Hughes, Everett C. "The Making of a Physician," Human Organ-
    ization, Vol. 14, No. 4 (Winter, 1956), pp. 21-25.

Huntington, Mary Jean. "Sociology of Professions, 1945-55," in
    Zetterberg, Hans L. (ed.), Sociology in the United States
    of America, Paris: UNESCO, 1956, pp. 87-93.

Kern, Fred, Jr. "An Experiment in Medical Education and Medical
    Care," American Journal of Public Health, Vol. 45, No. 1
    (Jan., 1955), pp. 47-52.

Lazarsfeld, Paul F., and Barton, Allen H. "Qualitative Measure-
    ment in the Social Sciences: Classification, Typologies
    and Indices," in Lerner, D., and Lasswell, H.D., (eds.),
    The Policy Sciences, Stanford: Stanford University Press,
    1951, pp. 155-92.

Lentz, Edith M. "The American Voluntary Hospital as an Example
    of Institutional Change," Unpublished Ph.D. dissertation,
    Cornell University, 1956.

Lentz, Edith M. "Hospital Administration - One of a Species,"
    Administrative Science Quarterly, Vol. 1, No. 4 (March,
    1957), pp. 444-63.

Levine, Gene N. "The Good Physician," Bureau of Applied Social
    Research, Columbia University, 1957 (mimeographed).

Levine, Gene N., Rogoff, Natalie, and Caplovitz, David.
    "Diversities in Role Conceptions," Bureau of Applied
    Social Research, Columbia University, 1955 (dittoed).

Lipset, Seymour M. "The Political Process in Trade Unions: A
    Theoretical Statement," in Berger, M., Abel, T., and Page,
    Charles H. (eds.), Freedom and Control in Modern Society,
    New York: Van Nostrand Co., 1954, pp. 82-124.

Lyman, Elizabeth L. "Occupational Differences in the Value
    Attached to Work," American Journal of Sociology, Vol. 61,
    No. 2 (Sept., 1955), pp. 138-44.

McEwen, William J. "Position Conflict and Professional Orien-
    tation in a Research Organization," Administrative Science
    Quarterly, Vol. 1, No. 2 (Sept., 1956), pp. 208-24.

Meltzer, Leo. "Scientific Productivity in Organizational
    Settings," Journal of Social Issues, Vol. 12, No. 2
    (1956), pp. 32-40.

Menzel, H., and Katz, Elihu. "Social Relations and Innovation in the Medical Profession: The Epidemiology of a New Drug," *Public Opinion Quarterly*, Vol. 19, No. 4 (Winter, 1956), pp. 337-54.

Merton, Robert K. "Selected Problems of Field Work in a Planned Community," *American Sociological Review*, Vol. 12, No. 3 (June, 1947), pp. 304-12.

Merton, Robert K. "Patterns of Influence: a Study of Interpersonal Influence and Communications Behavior in a Local Community," in Lazarsfeld, P.F., and Stanton, F.N. (eds.), *Communications Research, 1948-1949*, New York: Harper and Bros., 1949, pp. 180-219.

Merton, Robert K. "Some Preliminaries to a Sociology of Medical Education," in Merton, R.K. Reader, G.G., and Kendall, P.L. (eds.), *The Student-Physician*, Cambridge: Harvard University Press, 1957, pp. 3-79.

Merton, Robert K. "The Functions of the Professional Association," *American Journal of Nursing*, Vol. 58, No. 1 (Jan., 1958), pp. 50-54.

Merton, Robert K., Bloom, Samuel, and Rogoff, Natalie. "Studies in the Sociology of Medical Education," *Journal of Medical Education*, Vol. 31, No. 8 (August, 1956), pp. 552-64.

Page, Charles H. "Bureaucracy's Other Face," *Social Forces*, Vol. 25, No. 1 (Oct., 1946), pp. 88-93.

Page, Charles H. "Bureaucracy and Higher Education," *The Journal of General Education*, Vol. 5, No. 2 (Jan., 1951), pp. 91-100.

Parsons, Talcott. "Suggestions for a Sociological Approach to the Theory of Organizations - I," *Administrative Science Quarterly*, Vol. 1, No. 1 (June, 1956), pp. 63-85.

Parsons, Talcott. "Suggestions for a Sociological Approach to the Theory of Organizations - II," *Administrative Science Quarterly*, Vol. 1, No. 2 (Sept., 1956), pp. 225-39.

Pelz, Donald C. "Some Social Factors Related to Performance in a Research Organization," *Administrative Science Quarterly*, Vol. 1, No. 3 (Dec., 1956), pp. 310-25.

Reader, George G. "Comprehensive Medical Care," *Journal of Medical Education*, Vol. 28, No. 7 (July, 1953), pp. 34-40.

Reader, George G. "Organization and Development of a Comprehensive Care Program," American Journal of Public Health, Vol. 44, No. 6 (June, 1954), pp. 760-65.

Reader, George G. "Some of the Problems and Satisfactions of Teaching Comprehensive Medicine," Journal of Medical Education, Vol. 31, No. 8 (August, 1956), pp. 54-58.

Reader, George G. "The Cornell Comprehensive Care and Teaching Program," in Merton, R.K., Reader, G.G., and Kendall, P.L. (eds.), The Student-Physician. Cambridge: Harvard University Press, 1957, pp. 81-101.

Selznick, Philip. "An Approach to a Theory of Bureaucracy," American Sociological Review, Vol. 8, No. 1 (Feb., 1943), pp. 47-54.

Selznick, Philip. "Foundations of the Theory of Organization," American Sociological Review, Vol. 13, No. 1 (Feb., 1943), pp. 25-35.

Shepard, Herbert A. "The Value System of a University Research Group," American Sociological Review, Vol. 19, No. 4 (August, 1954), pp. 456-62.

Shepard, Herbert A. "Nine Dilemmas in Industrial Research," Administrative Science Quarterly, Vol. 1, No. 3 (Dec., 1956), pp. 295-309.

Shepherd, Clovis, and Brown, Paula. "Status, Prestige, and Esteem in a Research Organization," Administrative Science Quarterly, Vol. 1, No. 3 (Dec., 1956), pp. 340-60.

Smith, Harvey L. "The Sociological Study of Hospitals," Unpublished Ph.D. dissertation, University of Chicago, 1949.

Smith, Harvey L. "Two Lines of Authority are One Too Many," Modern Hospital, Vol. 84, No. 3 (March, 1955), pp. 59-64.

Tannenbaum, Arnold S., and Georgopoulos, Basil. "The Distribution of Control in Formal Organizations," Survey Research Center, University of Michigan (mimeographed, n.d.).

Trow, Martin. "Comment on 'Participant Observation and Interviewing: a Comparison," Human Organization, Vol. 16, No. 3 (Fall, 1957), pp. 33-35.

Wiguers, Richard T. "Who's on Top? Who Knows?", Modern Hospital, Vol. 86, No. 6 (June, 1956), pp. 51-54.

Wardwell, Walter I. "Social Integration, Bureaucratization, and the Professions," Social Forces, Vol. 33, No. 4 (May, 1955), pp. 356-59.

Watson, Goodwin (ed.), "Problems of Bureaucracy," Journal of Social Issues, Vol. 1, No. 4 (Dec., 1945).

Weiskotten, H.G., and Altenderfer, Marion E. "Trends in Medical Practice," Journal of Medical Education, Vol. 31, No. 7 (July, 1956), Part 2.

Wessen, Albert F. "The Social Structure of a Modern Hospital," Unpublished Ph.D. dissertation, Yale University, 1951.

Wilson, Robert N. "Teamwork in the Operating Room," Human Organization, Vol. 12, No. 4 (Winter, 1954), pp. 9-14.

Young, Donald. "Sociology and the Practicing Professions," American Sociological Review, Vol. 20, No. 6 (Dec., 1955), pp. 641-48.

Zetterberg, Hans L. "Compliant Actions," Acta Sociologica, Vol. 2, No. 4 (1957), pp. 179-201.

DISSERTATIONS ON SOCIOLOGY

An Arno Press Collection

Allison, Paul David. **Processes of Stratification in Science.** (Doctoral Dissertation, University of Wisconsin, 1976) 1980

Angell, Robert Cooley. **The Campus.** 1928

Bales, Robert Freed. **The "Fixation Factor" in Alcohol Addiction.** (Doctoral Dissertation, Harvard University, 1945) 1980

Barber, Bernard. **"Mass Apathy" and Voluntary Social Participation in the United States.** (Doctoral Dissertation, Harvard University) 1980

Beaver, Donald deB. **The American Scientific Community, 1800-1860.** (Doctoral Dissertation, Yale University, 1966) 1980

Becker, Howard S. **Role and Career Problems of the Chicago Public School Teacher.** (Doctoral Dissertation, University of Chicago, 1952) 1980

Birnbaum, Norman. **Social Structure and the German Reformation** (Doctoral Dissertation, Harvard University, 1957) 1980

Bittner, Egon. **Popular Interest in Psychiatric Remedies.** (Doctoral Dissertation, University of California, Los Angeles, 1961) 1980

Bredemeier, Harry C. **The Federal Public Housing Movement.** (Doctoral Dissertation, Columbia University, 1955) 1980

Breed, Warren. **The Newspaperman, News and Society** (Doctoral Dissertation, Columbia University, 1952) 1980

Caplovitz, David. **Student-Faculty Relations in Medical School** (Doctoral Dissertation, Columbia University, 1961) 1980

Clark, Burton R. **Adult Education in Transition.** 1956

Cohen, Steven Martin. **Interethnic Marriage and Friendship.** (Doctoral Dissertation, Columbia University, 1974) 1980

Cole, Stephen. **The Unionization of Teachers. 1969**

Costner, Herbert L. **The Changing Folkways of Parenthood.** (Doctoral Dissertation, Indiana University, 1960) 1980

Davis, Arthur K. **Thorstein Veblen's Social Theory.** (Doctoral Dissertation, Harvard University, 1941) With a New Foreword. 1980

Davis, Kingsley. **A Structural Analysis of Kinship.** (Doctoral Dissertation, Harvard University, 1936) 1980

Davison, W. Phillips. **The Berlin Blockade.** 1958

Devereux, Edward C., Jr. **Gambling and the Social Structure.** (Doctoral Dissertation, Harvard University, 1949) With a New Foreword. 1980

Duncan, Otis Dudley. **An Examination of the Problem of Optimum City Size.** (Doctoral Dissertation, University of Chicago, 1949) 1980

Elder, Glen H., Jr. **Family Structure and Socialization.** (Doctoral Dissertation, University of North Carolina, 1961) With a New Preface and Appendix Chapters. 1980

Etzioni, Amitai. **The Organizational Structure of the Kibbutz.** (Doctoral Dissertation, University of California, Berkeley, 1959) 1980

Friedman, Nathalie S. **Observability in School Systems.** (Doctoral Dissertation, Columbia University, 1968) 1980

Ginsberg, Ralph Bertram. **Anomie and Aspirations.** (Doctoral Dissertation, Columbia University, 1966) With a New Introduction and Appendix. 1980

Goode, Erich. **Social Class and Church Participation.** (Doctoral Dissertation, Columbia University, 1966) 1980

Goss, Mary E. Weber. **Physicians in Bureaucracy.** (Doctoral Dissertation, Columbia University, 1959) 1980

Hammond, Phillip Everett. **The Role of Ideology in Church Participation.** (Doctoral Dissertation, Columbia University, 1960) 1980

Hill, Robert Bernard. **Merton's Role Types and Paradigm of Deviance** (Doctoral Dissertation, Columbia University, 1969) 1980

Hyman, Herbert H. **The Psychology of Status.** (Doctoral Dissertation, Columbia University, 1942) 1942

Janowitz, Morris. **Mobility, Subjective Deprivation and Ethnic Hostility.** (Doctoral Dissertation, University of Chicago, 1948) 1980

Keller, Suzanne I. **The Social Origins and Career Lines of Three Generations of American Business Leaders.** (Doctoral Dissertation, Columbia University, 1953) 1980

Keyfitz, Nathan. **Urban Influence on Farm Family Size.** (Doctoral Dissertation, University of Chicago, 1952) 1980

Kohn, Melvin Lester. **Analysis of Situational Patterning in Intergroup Relations** (Doctoral Dissertation, Cornell University, 1952) 1980

Levine, Donald Nathan. **Simmel and Parsons.** (Doctoral Dissertation, University of Chicago, 1957) With a New Introduction. 1980

March, James G. **Autonomy as a Factor in Group Organization.** (Doctoral Dissertation, Yale University, 1953) With a New Introduction. 1980

Marsh, Robert M. **The Mandarins.** 1961

Moore, Wilbert E. **American Negro Slavery and Abolition.** 1971

Mullins, Nicholas C. **Social Networks among Biological Scientists** (Doctoral Dissertation, Harvard University, 1966) 1980

Nettler, Gwynne. **The Relationship between Attitude and Information Concerning the Japanese in America.** (Doctoral Dissertation, Stanford University, 1946) 1980

Nisbet, Robert A. **The Social Group in French Thought.** (Doctoral Dissertation, University of California, Berkeley, 1940) With a New Preface. 1980

O'Gorman, Hubert J. **Lawyers and Matrimonial Cases.** 1963

Reskin, Barbara F. **Sex Differences in the Professional Life Chances of Chemists.** (Doctoral Dissertation, University of Washington, 1973) With a New Introduction. 1980

Rosenberg, Morris. With the assistance of Edward A. Suchman and Rose K. Goldsen. **Occupations and Values.** 1957.

Rossi, Alice S. **Generational Differences in the Soviet Union.** (Doctoral Dissertation, Columbia University, 1957) 1980

Ryder, Norman B. **The Cohort Approach.** (Doctoral Dissertation, Princeton University, 1951) 1980

Schuessler, Karl F. **Musical Taste and Socio-Economic Background.** (Doctoral Dissertation, Indiana University, 1947) 1980

Short, James F., Jr. **An Investigation of the Relationship between Crime and Business Cycles.** (Doctoral Dissertation, University of Chicago, 1952) With a New Introduction. 1980

Sills, David L. **The Volunteers.** 1957.

Simmons, Roberta G. **An Experimental Study of the Role-Conflict of the First-Line Supervisor.** (Doctoral Dissertation, Columbia University, 1964) With a New Introduction. 1980

Skolnick, Jerome H. **The Stumbling Block.** (Doctoral Dissertation, Yale University, 1957) 1980

Storer, Norman W. **Science and Scientists in an Agricultural Research Organization.** (Doctoral Dissertation, Cornell University, 1961) 1980

Stouffer, Samuel A. **An Experimental Comparison of Statistical and Case History Methods of Attitude Research** (Doctoral Dissertation, University of Chicago, 1930) 1980

Strodtbeck, Fred L. **A Study of Husband-Wife Interaction in Three Cultures.** (Doctoral Dissertation, Harvard University, 1950) 1980

Swanson, Guy E. **Emotional Disturbance and Juvenile Delinquency** (Doctoral Dissertation, University of Chicago, 1948) 1980

Thielens, Wagner P., Jr. **The Socialization of Law Students.** (Doctoral Dissertation, Columbia University, 1965) 1980

Trow, Martin A. **Right-Wing Radicalism and Political Intolerance.** (Doctoral Dissertation, Columbia University, 1957) 1980

Vidich, Arthur J. **The Political Impact of Colonial Administration.** (Doctoral Dissertation, Harvard University, 1953) 1980

White, Harrison C. **Research and Development as a Pattern in Industrial Management.** (Doctoral Dissertation, Princeton University, 1960) 1980

Wright, Charles R. **The Effect of Training in Social Research on the Development of Professional Attitudes.** (Doctoral Dissertation, Columbia University, 1954) 1980

Wrong, Dennis H. **Class Fertility Trends in Western Nations.** (Doctoral Dissertation, Columbia University, 1956) 1980

Yinger, J. Milton. **Religion in the Struggle for Power.** 1946.